An ORESTEIA

TRANSLATED BY ANNE CARSON

ANNE CARSON was born in Canada and teaches Ancient Greek for a living. Her publications include *Eros the Bittersweet* (1986), *Glass, Irony and God* (1995), *Autobiography of Red: A Novel in Verse* (1998), *Economy of the Unlost* (1999), *The Beauty of the Husband: A Fictional Essay in 29 Tangos* (2001), *If Not, Winter: Fragments of Sappho* (2002), *Decreation: Poetry, Essays, Opera* (2005) and *Grief Lessons: Four Plays by Euripides* (2006).

T0048648

An ORESTEIA

AGAMEMNON BY AISKHYLOS

ELEKTRA BY SOPHOKLES

ORESTES BY EURIPIDES

An ORESTEIA

Translated by

ANNE CARSON

FARRAR, STRAUS AND GIROUX

NEW YORK

Farrar, Straus and Giroux
18 West 18th Street, New York 10011

The Library of Congress has cataloged the hardcover edition as follows:
An Oresteia / translated by Anne Carson. — 1st ed.
    p.   cm.
ISBN: 978-0-86547-902-9 (alk. paper)
    1. Greek drama (Tragedy)—Translations into English.   2. Agamemnon (Greek
mythology)—Drama.   3. Electra (Greek mythology)—Drama.   4. Orestes
(Greek mythology)—Drama.   I. Carson, Anne, 1950–   II. Aeschylus.
Agamemnon. English.   III. Sophocles. Electra. English.   IV. Euripides. Orestes.
English.

PA3626 .C37 2009
882'.0108—dc22

2009001420

Paperback ISBN: 978-0-86547-916-6

Designed by Ralph Fowler / rlfdesign

Our books may be purchased in bulk for promotional, educational, or business use.
Please contact your local bookseller or the Macmillan Corporate and Premium
Sales Department at 1-800-221-7945, extension 5442, or by e-mail at
MacmillanSpecialMarkets@macmillan.com.

www.fsgbooks.com

17 19 20 18

for Alice Cowan,

my first Greek teacher

CONTENTS

A NOTE FROM THE TRANSLATOR

Thunder only happens when it's raining.

—STEVIE NICKS

Not my idea to do this. It was the inspiration of the artistic director of the Classic Stage Company in New York City, Brian Kulick. Let me say how it came about.

I translated Sophokles' *Elektra* in 1987 and Euripides' *Orestes* in 2006 for different reasons: *Elektra* was commissioned by Oxford University Press for a series called *The Greek Tragedies in New Translations*; *Orestes* was presented as a staged reading at the 92nd Street Y in New York City. To translate Aiskhylos' *Agamemnon* had never crossed my mind. But in 2007 Brian Kulick approached me with the notion of trying my hand at *Agamemnon* and putting together an *Oresteia* that combined the three playwrights, which he would then undertake to produce. I said, "Who needs this?"—meaning, Aiskhylos has already given us an

Oresteia richer than rubies, of which lots of good translations exist. Why monkey around with it? But Kulick persisted in thinking it a good idea to make a non-foundational *Oresteia*. He spoke and wrote to me about this on several occasions. As I understand it, the project interested him first of all historically. To hear the same legend (the story of the house of Atreus) told by three different playwrights at three different vantage points of Athenian history would offer "a unique perspective on the Athenian moment," he said. Kulick saw a trajectory "from myth to mockery" in the three treatments.

> *In Aiskhylos' hands the story of the house of Atreus is designed to end in a valedictory celebration of Athenian democracy and its newborn sense of justice; when Sophokles takes over the tale it becomes more complex and contradictory; with Euripides the design is completely turned on its head. We follow a trajectory from myth to mockery. What happened to effect this? History happened. Aiskhylos composed his* Oresteia *shortly after Athens' victory at the battle of Marathon, which marked the height of Athenian military and cultural supremacy; Euripides finished his* Orestes *almost a hundred years later as Athens headed for ruin, due to her protracted involvement in the Peloponnesian War . . . The house of Atreus, for these tragedians, was a way of talking about the fate of Athens.*[1]

He was also intrigued by a stylistic differential in the three plays.

> *I always think of these three tragedians as being associated with different times of a metaphoric day. Aiskhylos is dawnlike, with iconic ideas, images, and action emerging into the light of consciousness. Euripides presents a twilight where everything is susceptible to tricks of a fading light, where tonalities are hard to grasp, where one moment is*

1. Brian Kulick, correspondence, somewhat adapted.

an azure sunset, the next a starless night. Between them, Sophokles,
under the glare of a noon sun that leaves nothing unexposed.[2]

You can see Brian was persuasive. Anyway, the idea of another
Oresteia grew on me, partly because I like big translation projects;
partly because it seems important to get Greek plays performed
more; partly because, as John Cage says, "There are things to hear
and things to see and that's what theater is."[3]

2. Ibid.

3. Richard Kostelanetz, ed., *John Cage: An Anthology* (New York: Da Capo Press,
1991), 22.

NUMBERING

For the convenience of the reader who may wish to check the English against the Greek text, or vice versa, the lines have been numbered according to both the Greek text and the translation. The lines of the English translation have been numbered in multiples of ten, and these numbers have been set in the right-hand margin. The (inclusive) Greek numeration will be found bracketed at the top of the page.

AGAMEMNON

by Aiskhylos

INTRODUCTION

It's like watching a forest fire. Big, violent, changing every minute and the sound not like anything else.

Every character in *Agamemnon* sets fire to language in a different way. Klytaimestra is a master of technologies, starting with the thousand-mile relay of beacons that brings news of the fall of Troy all the way from Asia to her in the first scene. She reenacts the relay in language that is so brilliant and so aggressive, she is like a conqueror naming parts of the world she now owns. She goes on to own everyone in the play—the chorus by argument and threat, Agamemnon by flattery and puns, Aigisthos by sexy cozening—with one exception. Kassandra she cannot conquer. Kassandra's defense, which is perfect, is silence. When Klytaimestra demands to know whether this foreign girl speaks Greek, Kassandra does not answer—for 270 lines (in the original text). Klytaimestra exits.

There is no reason why Kassandra should speak Greek. She is a Trojan princess who has never been away from home before. In fact, she will turn out to command all registers of this alien tongue—analytical, metaphoric, historical, prophetic, punning, riddling, plain as glass. But Apollo has cursed Kassandra. Her mind is foreign in a much deeper way. Although she sees every-

thing past, present and future, and sees it truly, no one ever be-
lieves what she says. Kassandra is a self-consuming truth. Aiskhylos sets her in the middle of his play as a difference you cannot
grasp, a glass that does not give back the image placed before it.

As a translator, I have spent years trying to grasp Kassandra in
words. Long before I had any interest in the rest of *Agamemnon*, I
found myself working and reworking the single scene in which
she appears with her language that breaks open. I got some fine
sentences out of it and thought to publish them, but this seemed
vain. I dreamed of her weirdly mixed with the winters of my
childhood and imagined a play where someone like Björk would
sing wild translingual songs while sailing down a snowy river of
ancient Asia Minor. But other people have tried such things and
anyway the play already exists. It is *Agamemnon*.

Eventually I accepted that what is ungraspable about Kassandra
has to stay that way. Aiskhylos has distilled into her in extreme
form his own method of work, his own way of using his mind,
his way of using the theater as a mind. The effect is well (if inad-
vertently) described by the painter Francis Bacon, who (talking
about his own method of painting) says:

> It seems to come straight out of what we choose to call the unconscious
> with the foam of the unconscious locked around it . . .

Francis Bacon makes his paintings, as Kassandra makes her
prophecies, by removing a boundary in himself. He wants to ac-
cess something more raw and real than the images articulated by
his conscious mind. Interestingly, he finds reading Aiskhylos especially conducive to this end:

> Reading translations of Aeschylus . . . opens up the valves of sensation
> for me.

Perhaps this is because Aiskhylos knows how to get these valves open too. Not just in the Kassandra scene but everywhere in *Agamemnon* there is a leakage of the metaphorical into the literal and the literal into the metaphorical. Images echo, overlap and interlock. Words are coined by pressing old words together into new compounds—"dayvisible" (54), "dreamvisible" (308), "manminded" (9), "thricegorged" (1116), "godaccomplished" (1127). Metaphors come, go and reappear as fact; for example, the figurative "dragnet of allenveloping doom" that the Greeks threw over Troy (267) materializes as the very real "dragnet—evil wealth of cloth" in which Klytaimestra snares Agamemnon to kill him (1138–39). Real objects are so packed with meanings both literal and metaphoric that they explode into symbol, like the red carpet or cloth over which Agamemnon walks as he enters his house (608–49).[1]

Francis Bacon says that his own images "work first upon sensation then slowly leak back into the fact,"[2] and he speaks of a need to "return fact onto the nervous system in a more violent way."[3] He means a violence deeper than subject matter:

> *When talking about the violence of paint, it's nothing to do with the violence of war. It's to do with an attempt to remake the violence of reality itself . . . the violence of suggestions within the image which can only be conveyed through paint . . . We nearly always live through*

---

1. Scholars do not agree on what this cloth is exactly—a carpet, several carpets, a pile of garments or just bolts of fabric. From what Agamemnon says, it is clear he thinks the cloth something exorbitant with which gods should be honored, not men. See J. D. Denniston and D. L. Page, eds., *Agamemnon* (New York: Oxford University Press, 1957), 148.

2. David Sylvester, *The Brutality of Fact: Interviews with Francis Bacon* (New York: Thames and Hudson, 1988), 56.

3. Ibid., 59.

screens—a screened existence. And I sometimes think, when people
say my work looks violent, that I have been able to clear away one or
two of the veils or screens.[4]

This violence is intrinsic to Aiskhylos' style. He uses language the
way Bacon uses paint, especially in the Kassandra scene where he
stages the working of her prophetic mind—the veils, the screens,
the violence, the clearing away. She is a microcosm of his
method.

Francis Bacon thinks of himself as a realist painter, although he
admits this requires him "to reinvent realism."[5] Aiskhylos is a realist too. They both have an instinct "to trap the living fact alive"
in all its messy, sensational, symbolic overabundance. Let's return
to the red carpet that Aiskhylos unrolls as if in slow motion in the
famous carpet scene (608–49) that carries Agamemnon into his
house and his death. This amazing red object can be interpreted
as blood, wealth, guilt, vengeance, impiety, female wile, male *hybris*, sexual seepage, bad taste, inexhaustible anger and an action
invented by Klytaimestra to break Agamemnon's will. As a wo-
ven thing, it reminds us that women are the ones who weave and
that weaving is an analogy for deceptiveness. Klytaimestra will
use cloth again when she snares Agamemnon to kill him. As a
red or purple-red object, the cloth is bloodlike but also vastly
expensive and ruined by trampling. Agamemnon fears that this
action will look insolent or impious or both—he feels all eyes
upon him. As a cause of dispute between husband and wife, the
red cloth unfolds her power to master him in argument and out-
wit him in battle. For this is a battle, and when he enters the
house, he has lost it. Notice he enters in silence while she comes
behind. Then she pauses and turns at the doorway to deliver one

4. Ibid., 82.
5. Ibid., 178.

of the most stunning speeches of the play ("There is the sea and who shall drain it dry?" 650ff.). It is a truism of ancient stagecraft that the one who controls the doorway controls the tragedy, according to Oliver Taplin.[6] In *Agamemnon* this is unmistakably Klytaimestra. The carpet scene is like a big red arrow Aiskhylos has painted on the play to underscore the fact.

Violence in *Agamemnon* emanates spectacularly from one particular word: justice. Notice how often this word recurs and how many different angles it has. Almost everyone in the play claims to know what justice is and to have it on their side—Zeus, Klytaimestra, Agamemnon, Aigisthos and (according to Kassandra) Apollo. The many meanings of the word *justice* have shaped the history of the house of Atreus into a gigantic double bind. No one can stop the vicious cycle of vengeance that carries on from crime to crime in its name. The bloodyfaced Furies are its embodiment. I don't think Aiskhylos wants to clarify the concept of justice in any final way, although lots of readers have seen this as the intention of his *Oresteia* overall. So far as *Agamemnon* goes, no definition is offered. The play shows that the word makes different sense to different people and how blinding or destructive it can be to believe your "justice" is the true one. This is not a problem with which we are unfamiliar nowadays. As Kassandra says, "I know that smell" (886, 983).

6. Oliver Taplin, *The Stagecraft of Aeschylus* (New York: Oxford University Press, 1977), 34, 280, 300, 307, 339–41.

DRAMATIS PERSONAE

(in order of appearance)

WATCHMAN

CHORUS   *of old men of Argos*

KLYTAIMESTRA   *wife of Agamemnon*

MESSENGER

AGAMEMNON   *king of Argos*

KASSANDRA   *Trojan princess, prophet,*
prisoner of war

AIGISTHOS   *paramour of Klytaimestra*

SETTING: *The play is set at the palace of Agamemnon, also known as the house of Atreus, in Argos. Agamemnon has been away for more than ten years at the Trojan War. It is the middle of the night. A watchman is lying on the palace roof.*

WATCHMAN   Gods! Free me from this grind!
            It's one long year I'm lying here watching
                waiting watching waiting—
            propped on the roof of Atreus, chin on my
                paws like a dog.
            I've peered at the congregation of the
                nightly stars—bright powerful creatures
                blazing in air,
            the ones that bring summer, the ones that
                bring winter,
            the ones that die out, the ones that rise
                up—
            and I watch I watch I watch for this sign of
                a torch,
            a beacon light sending from Troy the news
                that she is captured.
            Those are the orders I got from a certain
                manminded woman.
            But whenever I take to my restless dreamless
                dewdrenched bed   [10]
            I cannot close my eyes—fear stands over me
                instead of sleep.
            And whenever I think to sing or hum a
                tune to stay awake
            then my tears fall.

This house is in trouble.
The good days are gone.
How I pray for change! A happy change. A
    light in darkness.

[Light appears.]

Hold on! There you are! Fire in the night!
    Blazing like day!
You make me dance for joy!
I must send news to Agamemnon's wife to
    rise from bed, to shout aloud
for this amazing light—if Troy is really
    taken as the beacons seem to say.   [20]
I myself will start the dancing.
For if *they* are in luck, *I* am in luck—we're
    throwing triple sixes!
Oh how I long to see the master of this
    house and touch his hand!
For all the rest, I keep silent.
    Ox on my tongue.
This house if it could talk would tell a tale.
But me—I talk to those who know
and then
I lose my memory.

CHORUS   Ten years now since Priam's one great
                    adversary—
            Menelaos plus Agamemnon: twin royal
                    power sanctioned by Zeus—   [30]
        sent forth from this land a thousand ships to
                    fight their fight.

Loud was the cry—they screamed "War!" as
eagles scream
when they wheel in air and thrash their
wings for grief
high above the nests of children lost.
All that care lost.
But some god hears the cry, some Apollo or
Zeus or Pan,
and sooner or later sends down vengeance.
So it was Zeus—god of host, guest,
strangers, hospitality—
sent the sons of Atreus against Alexander
for the sake of a woman with too many
husbands.   [40]
There were heavy struggles and knees
pressed in the dust,
Trojan spears smashed and Greek spears
smashed.
Now things are where they are.
And will end where they're destined to end.
Not by burning things in secret, not by
libations poured in secret,
not by tears
will you turn away the wrath
of offerings that were unholy.
But we, old and useless as we are, left
behind by the army,
bide our time here, propped on
childstrength.   [50]
The marrow leaps not in our breast.
Ares is absent.
Old age goes its way withered, on three legs,

weak as a child or a dream dayvisible,
wavering.

But you,
daughter of Tyndareus, Queen Klytaimestra,
what's happened, what news, what rumor,
what message
persuades you to send round orders for
sacrifice?
All the altars in the city high and low,
heavenly and earthly,   [60]
blaze with offerings.
Everywhere torches shoot up to the sky,
coaxed by holy unguents and royal oils.
Tell what you can.
Heal my anxiety
for it flashes from darkness to hope
and chews me up inside.

Power comes into me!
I am breathed full by the gods
of strong song: [70]
how the two Atreid kings,
the twin command of Greece,
were sent with spears against the land of
Troy
by this one omen—
the king of birds appearing to the king of
ships.
A black eagle and behind it a white one,
whirling in the open air
to drop upon a pregnant hare.

They ate the hare, they ate her womb, they
ate her unborn young.
Sing sorrow, sorrow, but let the good prevail.   [80]

Then the prophet of the army
saw the haredevouring birds were two,
saw the warmongering Atreids were two,
and he unfolded the omen:
In time this expedition will capture Priam's city,
will slaughter all its cattle before its walls.
Only let no hatred from the gods darken down
upon this army—
this bridle forced onto the mouth of Troy.
For holy Artemis you know feels pity and anger
at the predators of Zeus who fell upon a cringing
hare.   [90]
She hates the feast of the eagles.
Sing sorrow, sorrow, but let the good prevail.

Gracious as she is to the tender cubs of lions,
delighting as she does in savage beasts still
helpless at the breast,
she calls out for this omen to be realized—
both its favor and its blame.
But I pray Apollo will prevent her
raising adverse winds to keep the Greeks from
sailing:
she wants to instigate another sacrifice,
a lawless joyless strifeplanting sacrifice   [100]
that will turn a wife against a husband.
For there lives in this house
a certain form of anger,

a dread devising everrecurring everremembering
anger
that longs to exact vengeance for a child.
So spoke Kalchas to the kings.
Sing sorrow, sorrow, but let the good prevail.

Zeus! whoever Zeus is—
if he likes this name I'll use it—
measuring everything that exists I can
compare with Zeus nothing   [110]
except Zeus.
May he take this weight from my heart.
The god who was great before Zeus
is not worth mentioning now.
The one who came after that is past and
gone.
Zeus is the victor! Proclaim it:
bull's-eye!

Zeus put mortals on the road to wisdom
when he laid down this law:
By suffering we learn.   [120]
Yet there drips in sleep before my heart
a griefremembering pain.
Good sense comes the hard way.
And the grace of the gods
(I'm pretty sure)
is a grace that comes by violence.

So then
the captain of the Greek ships,
blaming no prophet,

chose to veer along with the blasts of
fortune.   [130]
His men could not sail,
his men were starving,
on the shore of Chalcis in the region of
Aulis
where the roaring tides go back and forth.

Winds from the north came
bringing idle time they did not want,
bringing hunger and days at anchor enough
to drive men mad,
sparing neither ships nor cables,
every minute longer than the last,
grinding this flower of Greek men to
nothing.   [140]
And the seer cried out *Artemis!*—an answer
more bitter than the question.
The sons of Atreus smote the ground and
wept.

And Agamemnon spoke:
Hard for me to disobey.
Hard for me to cut down my own daughter,
prize of my house,
defiling a father's hand with a girl's blood at the
altar.
Which of these is apart from evil?
How can I desert my ships and fail my allies?   [150]
Their desperation cries out for a sacrifice to change
the winds,
a girl must die.

It is their right.
May the good prevail!

Then he put on the yoke of Necessity.
His mind veered toward unholiness,
his nerve turned cold.
It is delusion makes men bold,
knocks them sideways,
causes grief.   [160]
Sacrificer of his own daughter he became.
To further a war fought for a woman.
To pay off his ships.

Her prayers and cries of *Father!* her young
life
they reckoned at zero,
those warloving captains.
Her father said a prayer and bid them seize
her
high above the altar like a goat
with her face to the ground and her robes
pouring around her.
And on her lovely mouth—   [170]

to check the cry that would have cursed his
house—
he fixed a bridle.
Her robe fell to the ground.
She cast a glance at each of her killers,
like a figure in a painting speaking with her
eyes,

for she used to sing to them around her
       father's table.
blessing their libation in her pure girl's
       voice—

what happened then I did not see and
       cannot tell.
    Let's just say Kalchas was no liar.
Justice tips her scales so that we learn by
       suffering.   [180]
But the future—who knows? It's here soon
       enough.
      Why grieve in advance?
Whatever turns up, I hope it's happy—

[Enter KLYTAIMESTRA.*]*

    in accord with *her* wishes,
   our one-woman citadel and bulwark.

I am here to reverence your power,
    Klytaimestra.
When the king is away one must honor
    the queen.
So you got good news?
You're optimistic?
Tell me, unless you don't want to.   [190]

KLYTAIMESTRA   Good news. Joy surpassing all your hopes!
    The Greeks have captured Priam's
    town!

CHORUS   What do you say? I can't take it in!

KLYTAIMESTRA   Troy belongs to us! Clear?

CHORUS   My tears fall for joy.

KLYTAIMESTRA   Your eye is loyal.

CHORUS   And is there proof? Have you evidence?

KLYTAIMESTRA   I have. Unless some god fooled me.

CHORUS   You're persuaded by visions in dreams?

KLYTAIMESTRA   I would not trust a mind asleep.

CHORUS   Some rumor then?   [200]

KLYTAIMESTRA   You think me a child?

CHORUS   When was the city destroyed?

KLYTAIMESTRA   In the night, this past night.

CHORUS   What messenger could come so fast?

KLYTAIMESTRA   Hephaistos, god of fire! He sped forth a
                blazing flame from Ida!
                Beacon after beacon as the fire messenger
                moved
                from Ida to the rock of Lemnos

to the crag of Athos third,
and skimming high above the sea it shot
   across like joy,
the burning pine torch as another sun,   [210]
to the watcher on Makistos,
who delayed not, nor was he asleep,
so the beacon sent its sign
to sentinels of Messapion who lit a heap of
   heather
and sped the message on. Not yet growing
   dim
it leapt the plain of Asopos
bright as a moon to the cliff of Kithairon
and roused a successor of sending flame,
which the watchers did not ignore but
   made an even bigger blaze
that flashed over the Gorgon's lake and
   reached Mount Aigiplanktos   [220]
urging the mandate of fire further.
Then they kindled a huge beard of flame
that overleapt the Saronic Gulf
and swooped down bright upon the peak of
   Arachnaios,
nextdoor neighbor to us here,
and plunged at last onto the roof of
   Atreus—this fire
that traveled all the way from Ida.
This was my lightbringing strategy,
torch to torch over the entire course.
Victory for both the first and the last.   [230]
Such is the proof and evidence I offer you,

sent by my husband
from Troy to me
personally.

CHORUS   To the gods I will give thanks, lady, later.
But tell me your whole story uninterrupted.
I am amazed.

KLYTAIMESTRA   Troy is ours on this day.
Within that city, I imagine, sounds a cry
          that does not blend—
oil and water poured together do not like
          each other,   [240]
you could say, they stand aloof.
So the voices of vanquished and victor are
          distinct upon the ear.
Some fall on the bodies of their husbands,
          fathers, brothers
and cry out grief from throats no longer
          free.
The others, famished after allnight battle,
          search for any breakfast they can find.
No billets, no order, just chance.
But quartered now in captured Trojan
          homes, escaped from frost and dew,
they'll sleep like happy men the whole
          night through without a watch.
And if only they reverence the gods and
          temples of that city
these captors will not fall captive in turn.   [250]
Let no mad impulse strike the army to
          ravish what they should not,

overcome by greed.

They're not home yet.

Yet even if they make it home without
    offending gods

the agony of those who died may
    wake again—I pray no sudden

shift to evil.

Such are my woman words.

May the good prevail.

Unambiguously.

I'm ready for blessings, *many* blessings.   [260]

CHORUS   Woman, you talk like a sensible man.

Now that I've heard your proofs—and
    they're good proofs—

I shall address the gods with gratitude
    for our success.

O Zeus king, O night of glory
you have thrown over the towers of Troy
a net so vast no man could overleap it,
a dragnet of allenveloping doom.
I reverence great Zeus, the god of host
    and guest
who bent his bow against Paris
    and did not miss.   [270]

People talk about "the stroke of Zeus."
Trace the meaning.
Zeus acts as Zeus ordains.
Do you think the gods ignore a man who
    steps on holy things?

That man is impious
whose daring goes beyond justice,
who packs his house with wealth in excess.
Now me, I'm a moderate person.
But a man of excess has no shelter.
He kicks the altar of Justice out of sight.   [280]

Persuasion drives him on—she is child of
ruin.
There is no cure. The damage is plain—
it shines like bad bronze, black on the
touchstone.
Like a boy lost in dreams
such a man brings disgrace on his city.
No god hears his prayers
and if you befriend him, Justice will
take you down.
Such a man is Paris, who came to the house
of Atreus
and outraged his host
by stealing his wife—   [290]

Helen who bequeathed to her people
clang of shields,
press of spears,
throng of ships.
Helen who brought ruin to Troy instead of
a dowry.
Lightly, lightly, she went through the gates
and the seers wailed aloud:
Alas for the house! Alas for the house and the
men of the house!

Alas for the marriage bed and the way she loved
her husband once!
There is silence there: he sits alone,   [300]
dishonored, baffled, mute.
In his longing for what is gone across the
sea
a phantom seems to rule his house.
Any image of her is hateful to him.
Without her eyes
all Aphrodite is gone.

Dreams bring him grief or delusional joy—
dreamvisible she slips through his hands and
never comes back
down the paths of sleep.
Such is the sorrow throughout that house.   [310]
But grief sits at the hearth of every house
where a man sailed off to war.
Many things pierce a woman's heart:
in place of the man she sent out
she knows
she'll get back
a handful of ash.

Ares
who exchanges bodies for gold,
Ares who holds the scales of war,   [320]
sends home to the wife
the dust of her man
packed in an easy little urn.
And the lament goes: *What a master of battle*
he was!

How beautifully he died! while some people
snarl under their breath
All for the sake of another man's wife!
in resentment against the Atreidai, those
champions of justice.
And what about those who lie *over there*—
under the ground at Troy,
planted in enemy soil?

The citizens' talk is heavy with anger. They
want to see a penalty paid.   [330]
I'm anxious—I'm not sure what lurks in the
dark.
Certainly the gods see all this killing.
And the Furies destroy a man who prospers
unjustly,
they grind his life away to nothing.
Dangerous to be big or famous—
there strikes the thunderbolt of Zeus!
I prefer to remain obscure.
I'm no sacker of cities!
Let me keep
my little life to myself.   [340]

But this beacon sends rumor racing through
the town.
Is it true? Who knows? Some lie sent by
gods?
What man is so childish or daft
that his mind takes fire at news of a beacon
then falls to despair
if a word is changed?

On the other hand
　　isn't it just like a woman
to want to rejoice before anything is clear.
　　The female skin is much too porous.   [350]
　　And her gossip dies in a day.

Well, soon we'll know about these lights
　　and fires and beacons,
whether they're true or just some fantasy.
But look, I see a messenger coming from
　　the shore,
branches of olive on his head.
Covered in thirsty dust.
This man will make things clear—using
　　words, not fire and smoke.
He'll tell us whether to celebrate or—*or
　　what* I don't like to say.

[Enter MESSENGER.*]*

MESSENGER　　I greet you, ground of my fathers, land of
　　Argos.
In this tenth-year light I come to you.   [360]
Many hopes are shattered, one is left:
I never dreamed that at my death I'd be
　　buried in the place I love best.
Rejoice my homeland,
rejoice light of the sun,
and you highest Zeus and you Pythian
　　Apollo—
may you launch no more arrows against
　　us.

You were hostile enough on the banks of
    Skamander, Apollo, now our savior!
I greet all the gods here, especially Hermes
    patron of messengers.
You who sent us out, welcome us home,
    this remnant of the army.
O royal halls, O beloved roof, O holy seats
    and gods that face the sun,   [370]
receive your king with glad eyes at last.
He is come, bringing light in darkness,
    Agamemnon.
Welcome him well for he deserves it,
he has dug up Troy with the shovel of Zeus,
    the shovel of Justice.
The soil of Troy is worked down to nothing.
Her altars are vanished, her temples are
    gone.
The seed of the land is utterly desolate.
Such a yoke did our king throw around
    Troy!
And now he is home, a blessed man,
worthy of honor beyond all the living.   [380]
Neither Paris nor Troy
can boast their deed was greater than their
    suffering.
That rapist-robber lost his plunder
and razed his father's house to the ground.
Double the price did the sons of Priam pay
    for their crime.

CHORUS   Glad welcome to you, messenger of the
    army.

MESSENGER   Glad indeed. If gods want me to die, I'm
            ready now.

CHORUS   Did longing for your home afflict you
            there?

MESSENGER   Oh yes, oh yes, so that my eyes are filled
            with tears.

CHORUS   A sweet affliction then.   [390]

MESSENGER   How so?

CHORUS   The feeling was reciprocal.

MESSENGER   You mean you longed for the army?

CHORUS   Oh often we sighed from a dark heart.

MESSENGER   Why dark?

CHORUS   Silence is the only safe answer to that.

MESSENGER   You've come to fear someone?

CHORUS   Let me borrow your words: I'm ready to die.

MESSENGER   Yes, but it's over now.
            And as for all that happened all those
                years—some of it happy,   [400]
            some of it not—well, who is free from
                suffering except the gods?

Were I to tell you our hardships—the
    miserable quarters,
narrow gangways, lousy beds and how we
    groaned on days there was no food!—
but it was worse onshore.
Our beds right up against the enemy walls.
Rain from the sky, dew from the ground
    soaking us perpetually,
rotting our clothes, filling our hair with
    vermin.
I could tell you stories of winter so cold it
    killed the birds in the air.
Or summer heat when the sea at noon lay
    without a crease—
but why bewail this? Our toil is past. Over.   [410]
The dead do not care to rise again.
Why should I count them?
Why pick at old wounds? Goodbye grief!
For us, this remnant of army, it feels like a
    victory!
So here is our boast: we took Troy finally
and nailed plunder to the walls of Greece
    to glorify our gods.
Praise the city and the generals, you who
    hear this.
And the grace of Zeus that brought the
    thing to pass.
That's my whole story.

CHORUS   You prove me wrong, I don't deny.   [420]
    Never too old to learn.
    But all this concerns Klytaimestra most.

KLYTAIMESTRA I raised my shout of joy a while ago,
              when the fire first blazed through the night,
                  announcing Troy's fall.
              There were of course those who rebuked
                  me saying,
              "You've convinced yourself that Troy is
                  sacked because of *a beacon*!
              How like a woman!" They called me
                  insane.
              Well, I went on with my offerings:
                  all through the city
              women raised the women's cry of jubilation
                  in the temples of the gods,
              throwing spices on the flames. And now,
                  what need for you to tell me more?   [430]
              From the king himself I shall learn
                  everything—how best to welcome him
                  oh I'm excited—
              what day is sweeter for a wife
              than when she runs to open the door
                  for her husband back from war?—
              bring him this message: come with all
                  speed, you darling of the city.
              You'll find your loyal wife just as you
                  left her,
              guarding the house like a good dog,
              enemy to your enemies,
              quite unchanged.
              She broke no seal while you were away.
              And she knows no more of secret sex
                  or scandal   [440]
              than she does of dipping bronze.

This is my boast.
It's one hundred percent true and worthy
    of a king's wife.

CHORUS   That's how she talks. You may need an
    intepreter.
But tell me, messenger, what of Menelaos?
Did he come back safe with you?

MESSENGER   Would that I could lie!

CHORUS   Would the truth were happy!

MESSENGER   He vanished from the army, he
    and his ship too.

CHORUS   You saw him leave Troy? Or did some storm
    snatch him?   [450]

MESSENGER   That's it, you hit the mark.

CHORUS   And they call him alive or dead?

MESSENGER   No one knows.

CHORUS   Describe the storm.

MESSENGER   I don't like to mar a joyful day with
    unwelcome news.
It's like mixing two different gods.
When a longfaced messenger comes to a
    city bringing tales of its army fallen,

of a wound cut into the flesh of the people,
of men from every house thrown onto
   the bloody prong of Ares,
it's appropriate he sings out a hymn
   to the Furies.   [460]
But when he comes bringing victory to a
   city of joy—how can I mix evil into that?
How tell of the storm that fell on the
   Argives from angry gods?
For Fire and Water swore an oath—eternal
   enemies before—
to wreck our fleet.
Steep ruinous oceans rose by night, winds
   lunged out of Thrace and dashed
the ships on one another.
The water went wild. Ships simply
   vanished.
Like sheep lost to a floundering shepherd.
When dawn came we saw the Aigian Sea
   abloom with bodies and pieces of wreck.
Some devious god kept us and our hull
   intact,   [470]
some forgiving god, with a nudge of the
   tiller.
Salvation took its seat on our boat and we
   did not go under, nor run up onshore.
No—we swept out of death into sudden
   bright daylight scarcely trusting our luck,
then took account of a new cataclysm—our
   fleet in shreds.
If any man of them still breathes, of course
   he thinks us lost, as we do him.

May it turn out well!
As for Menelaos, expect him.
Some ray of light may find that man alive,
if Zeus is not yet inclined to wipe out his
    family,
there's hope he'll come home.   [480]
That's the truth.

CHORUS   Who can have named her so perfectly?
                    What prophetic mind?
            Who was it gave to that bride of blood, that
                wife of strife, the name *Helen*? For the
            woman is hell to ships, hell to men, hell to
                    cities.
            She vanished out the veils of her bedroom
                    on a western wind
                and in her wake came men with shields
                    tracking her all the way
            to the shore of Troy. They beached in
                    blood.

            Trouble came to Troy. It had the name
                wedding, it had the name *funeral*.
            It began in dishonoring Zeus, god of the
                    feast
            where her wedding song was sung.
                    Wrongfully sung.   [490]
            Then Troy grew old overnight. Troy
                    changed its tune
                to one of sorrow. Paris became the
                    bridegroom of doom.

And Helen made misery and death for her
people just by living among them.

A man reared a lion cub once in his house.
It was new at the breast,
a young gentle thing, tumbling and playing
with children, delighting the old. The man
took it up in his arms
like an infant, nuzzling his hand when its
belly was empty.

But time passed. It started to show its lion
nature—
made an uninvited feast of slaughtered
sheep,
spilling blood and havoc from room to
room.   [500]
That thing was a priest of ruin. Bred in the
house. Sent by god.

At first, I think, there came to Troy a spirit
of windless calm.
An ornament—a pretty glance, little sting to
the heart.
But she swerved aside to a marriage of
murder and tears.
She harmed the place, she harmed the
people, she was sent by Zeus
to the city of Priam: bride as disaster. Bride
as Fury.

You know the old saying—Great wealth
gives birth to great woe.
Now here is my own opinion:
One unholy deed breeds another unholy
deed.   [510]
A righteous house has righteous children.

Old *hybris* makes new *hybris*.
In the hour of crisis
you cannot resist her, you cannot fight
back—
an utter unholy recklessness will take you
and curse you and ruin your house.
Like mother, like child.

But Justice shines in shabby houses
and honors the virtuous life.
From golddrenched halls and unclean hands
she turns away—toward holiness. Not
wealth, not pomp, not praise.   [520]
Justice guides us all.

[*Enter* AGAMEMNON, *with* KASSANDRA
behind at a distance.]

CHORUS   Enter king, sacker of Troy, son of Atreus—
how should I address you?
How can I show you just the right amount
of deference and courtesy?
Many people cherish a show of feeling.
They're quite wrong.

You can always find someone to groan
    along with your misfortune
(while the sting doesn't reach his heart)
or join in your joy (note the fake smile).
But no smart shepherd is deceived by a
    fawning flock or its watery love.
Now I have to admit when you sent an
    army after Helen
I wrote you off as a loose cannon.   [530]
But I also admit, you did it! You won!
And you'll learn in time
if you ask the right questions
who kept your city safe for you and who
    did not.

AGAMEMNON   First Argos and the gods of Argos
I think it right to greet—those gods
who had a share in my return and the
    justice I took from Priam's town.
They didn't wait for legal arguments but
    cast their vote straight into the urn of
    blood.
So much for Troy.
There was an urn of hope but it was
    empty.   [540]
Look, smoke still floats above that city,
    you can see it.
Storms of ruin there. The ashes stink
    with wealth.
For this victory we must pay the gods
    everlasting gratitude.

We threw a noose around Troy's arrogance
   and—for a woman's sake—
ground the city to powder.
We are the wild beast of Argos,
descended from horses, sheathed in shields,
   that overleapt the towers of Troy,
a rawflesheating lion to lap the blood of
   kings!

That's what I have to say to the gods.
Now you (old men): I hear and I agree with
   your anxieties.   [550]
I see your point.
Few men can praise a friend's success
   without resentment—
there is a poison settles on the heart and
   makes it twice as painful
when a man in distress has to look on
   another rejoicing.
I know. I am acquainted with the mirror
   of society—
why, all those men who posed as loyal
   friends to me?
No more than ghosts or shadows.
Odysseus alone turned out to be a steady
   tracehorse—
alive or dead as he may be.
For all the rest: we'll call an assembly.
   Deliberate.   [560]
Where things go well, we'll plan how to
   prolong it.

Where there is need of medicine and
    healing, we'll cauterize or cut.
Clear out that disease!
So now into my house, my hearth, and
    greet the gods.
They sent me forth, they bring me back.
May Victory, who came with me, abide and
    stay.

KLYTAIMESTRA   Gentlemen, citizens, elders of Argos, you,
I am not ashamed to tell you of my
    husbandloving ways.
Shyness diminishes with age.
The fact is, life got hard for me when he
    was off at Troy.   [570]
It's a terrible thing for a woman to sit alone
    in a house,
listening to rumors and tales of disaster
    one after another arriving—
why, had this man sustained as many
    wounds as people told me,
he'd be fuller of holes than a net!
To die as often as they reported he'd need
    three bodies
and three cloaks of earth—one for each
    burial.
So often did nasty rumors reach me,
I hung up a noose for my neck more than
    once.
Other people had to cut me down.
That's why our boy—yours and mine—

Orestes, is not standing here, as he
  should be.   [580]
Don't worry. Strophios has him,
our Phokian ally, who warned me of
  problems,
your danger beneath Troy but also anarchy
  at home—
the people throwing off your government.
They love to kick a man who's down.
I'm telling the truth. This is not an excuse.
As for me,
my torrents of tears have dried away.
Not one drop left.
My poor eyes ache with weeping and
  watching all the night—   [590]
I watched for those beacon fires myself.
  No one else kept vigil as I did.
And the lightest buzzing of a gnat would
  wake me if I fell into a dream.
There I saw you catastrophized in more
  ways than there were moments of sleep.
So now, with all that over, with my mind
  grief free,
I salute my man: he is the watchdog
  of the palace,
forestay of the ship,
pillar of the roof,
only son of his father,
land appearing to sailors lost at sea,
fine weather after storms,   [600]
fresh stream to a thirsty traveler.
Is it not sweet to escape necessity!

We've had our share of evils!
Envy begone!

And now, dear one, as a special favor to me,
I pray you descend from your car without
     setting foot on the ground—
O King, this foot that wasted Troy!

[To servants.]

What are you waiting for? You have your
     orders—strew the ground with fabrics,
     now!
Make his path crimsoncovered!
     purplepaved! redsaturated!
So Justice may lead him to the home he
     never hoped to see.   [610]
Everything else I'll arrange myself with my
     usual sleepless vigilance—
exactly right, gods willing.

AGAMEMNON   Offspring of Leda, guard of my house, you
               have made a speech to match my
               absence—
               long.
               But praise of me should come from
               others.
               Don't pamper me with female ways, don't
                    fuss like some groveling barbarian,
               don't strew my path with anything at all!
                    You'll draw down envy.
               That stuff is for gods.

I am mortal. I can't trample luxuries
    underfoot. Honor me as a man
    not a divinity.
Anyway, who needs red carpets—my fame
    shouts aloud.   [620]
Here discretion is key.
Count no man happy until he dies happy.
If I keep this rule, I'll be okay.

KLYTAIMESTRA   Oh come on, relax your principles.

AGAMEMNON   No I will not. My principles are firm.

KLYTAIMESTRA   Would you have done it for the gods to
    satisfy a vow?

AGAMEMNON   Yes, if some religious expert prescribed it.

KLYTAIMESTRA   What about Priam, if he'd won the war?

AGAMEMNON   Oh Priam would love to walk on stuff like
    this.

KLYTAIMESTRA   Still you fear the blame of common men?   [630]

AGAMEMNON   The voice of the people does have power.

KLYTAIMESTRA   Unenvied means unenviable, you know.

AGAMEMNON   You're like a bulldog. It's not very feminine.

KLYTAIMESTRA   Yet a winner must acknowledge his victory.

AGAMEMNON   And you insist on this victory?

KLYTAIMESTRA   Yes! I do! Bend to me. Please!

AGAMEMNON   Oh all right. Let someone loose my sandals,
                    good slaves of my feet.
             and as I tread upon these crimson cloths
             let no evil eye of envy from the gods strike
                    down on me.
             What a shame to trample the wealth of the
                    house   [640]
             and ruin fabrics worth their weight in silver.
             Well, so it goes.
             Take this foreign girl into the house.
             Treat her kindly.
             God looks graciously upon a gentle
                    master—and no one wants to be a slave.
             She is choice plunder, picked out for me by
                    the army, my companion on the way.
             And now, since I am compelled to do your
                    will,
             I shall proceed into the house
             walking on red carpets.

             [Exit AGAMEMNON.]

KLYTAIMESTRA   There is the sea and who shall drain it dry?   [650]
             It breeds the purple stain, the dark red dye
                    we use to color our garments,
             costly as silver.
             This house has an abundance. Thanks
                    be to gods, no poverty here.

Oh I would have vowed the trampling of
    many cloths
if an oracle had ordered it, to ransom this
    man's life.
For when the root is alive the leaves come
    back
and shade the house against white dogstar
    heat.
Your homecoming is warmth in winter.
Or when Zeus makes wine from bitter
    grapes
and coolness fills the house   [660]
as the master walks his halls,
righteous, perfect.
Zeus, Zeus, god of things perfect,
accomplish my prayers.
Concern yourself here.
Perfect *this*.

CHORUS   Why does this fear
                float
        always in front of my heart—
          hungry for signs of the future—   [670]
singing a prophetic song no one asked for
           or paid for?
    Why can't I thrust it off like a difficult
            dream?
    My confidence drains away from the center
           of me.
    Yet it was years ago the Greek ships tossed
      their ropes on the beach at Troy

and I saw them come home with my
own eyes.
Still at the edge of my heart the song of the
Furies keeps nagging—
no one taught me this song and it has no
music,
all the same it shakes me.
My thoughts go round and round.   [680]
I know it all means something real but I
hope not! I pray not!

Health and disease collaborate, don't they?
They share a wall between.
So a man's fortune runs a straight course
then strikes a hidden reef.
Yet if as a precaution
we throw overboard a certain measure of
wealth,
our house doesn't sink,
our ship sails on
and Zeus keeps sending up field after field
of grain to stave off famine.   [690]

But the black blood of a man
once it falls to the ground
who can call it back?
Even the healer who thought he knew how
was checked by Zeus.
I am a restrained person.
Otherwise my heart would race past my
tongue to pour out everything.
Instead I mumble,

I gnaw myself.
I lose hope.   [700]
And my mind is burning.

[Enter KASSANDRA.*]*

KLYTAIMESTRA   Get yourself into the house, I'm talking to
you, Kassandra.
Now that Zeus has enrolled you in our
household,
made you a sharer of our water,
take your stand by the altar with the other
slaves.
Come on, get down here, don't be proud.
They say even Herakles once was sold
as a slave,
ate slave's bread.
And if that is your lot, lucky you—your
masters here are solid old money.
New money people are rough on servants.   [710]
Now you know what to expect.

CHORUS   *[To* KASSANDRA.*]* Your turn. She's
talking to you.
You're not a free person:
you'll obey her of course. Or maybe
you won't.

KLYTAIMESTRA   Does she talk only "barbarian"—those
weird bird sounds?
Does she have a brain?

CHORUS   [*To* KASSANDRA.] Your best option is to go
                    with her.
               Do as she says. Go.

KLYTAIMESTRA   I can't waste time like this in the doorway.
               Already the animals stand at the hearth
                    ready for slaughter—   [720]
               a joy we never hoped to see.
               So you get a move on, or you'll miss
                    the whole ceremony.
               If you really don't understand a word I'm
                    saying
               make some sign with your hand.

CHORUS   Of an interpreter she seems, this stranger, to
                    have need.
               For her way of turning is that of a
                    newcaught animal's.

KLYTAIMESTRA   Oh she's mad. Hearkens only to her own
                    mad mind.
               Brought from a captured city yet she knows
                    not how to take the bit—
               she frets her inside mouth away in foam of
                    blood.
               I'll not be insulted further.   [730]

               [*Exit* KLYTAIMESTRA.]

CHORUS   But I, for I pity you, will not get angry.
               Poor creature, come down from there.

Here is necessity. Here is a yoke for you to
bear.

KASSANDRA   OTOTOI POPOI DA!
              Apollo!
                  O!pollo!
                      Woepollo!
                          O!

CHORUS   Why do you mix up Apollo with "woe"?
           This god does not ever near sorrow go.   [740]

KASSANDRA   OTOTOI POPOI DA!
              Apollo!
                  O!pollo!
                      Woepollo!
                          O!

CHORUS   She calls on the god in an unlucky way.
           This god has no part in anyone's death day.

KASSANDRA   Apollo
              Apollo
                  god of the ways   [750]
                      god of my ruin oh
                          yes you destroy me oh
                              yes it is absolute this time

CHORUS   She looks about to prophesy and tell her
           side.
           The god is stretching a slave's mind wide.

KASSANDRA   Apollo
        Apollo
           god of the ways
              god of my ruin where
                  have you brought me what   [760]
                  house have you got me to

CHORUS   The house of Atreus, look and you'll see.
You can trust me.

KASSANDRA   Godhated so
        then too
           much knowing together self-
              murder man-
                chop blood-
                  slop floor

CHORUS   She's keen as a hound tracking a smell.   [770]
She'll find blood, she'll tell.

KASSANDRA   Evidence
        evidence
          here
          they shriek children
            roasted on spits a
              father-
              gorged live—
                  flesh-
                    feast   [780]

CHORUS   Of course we've heard of your talents
before.

But we're not in the market for prophets
anymore.

KASSANDRA   *[scream]* what
        [scream] how
            [scream] what in the world
                is this *[scream]* strange
                     new *[scream]*
                big as the house
              evil in the house
         who can lift it who can heal it   [790]
     help is a world away

CHORUS   Some of this I don't get.
        Some of it is old hat.

KASSANDRA   *[scream]* woman
        will you
            wash your man in the bath
           how can I
              soon it will
                there she goes
                   hand over hand is   [800]
                     reaching
                       out

CHORUS   Riddles all together with oracles tossed.
        I'm still lost.

KASSANDRA   *[scream] [scream] [scream] [scream]* what is this
        appearing a
        net of hell no

       the wife is the net he's
         married to murder here
           comes insatiable vengeance
    howling the sacrifice
        into   [810]
        place

CHORUS   Who is this spirit of vengeance you call to?
        Your words make me falter.
        It races my heart the yellow fear
        as when death is near.

KASSANDRA   *[scream] [scream]* look
       there look
        there keep
          the bull from the cow she
               nets him she gores
                  him with [820]
           her deadly black
              horn he
         falls he's
       down he bathes in
      death are you listening to
      me

CHORUS   Prophecy usually goes right over my head.
        Still it sounds grim what she said.
        Oh what good do prophets ever bring?
        They tinge with terror the simplest thing.   [830]

KASSANDRA   *[scream] [scream]* evil life evil luck evil I
        am just this sound look the

cup of my pain is already poured
out why
did you bring me
here was
it for this
was it for this
was it for

CHORUS   You're mad—godstruck godswept
godnonsensical   [840]
and you keep making that sound, it's not
musical.
Like the nightingale who wails her lost
child, you're inexhaustibly wild.
Sorrow this, sorrow that,
sorrow this, sorrow that.

KASSANDRA   But yes think oh think of the clear
nightingale—
gods put round her a wing
a life with no sting
but for me waits
schismos
of the double-edged sword: *schismos*
means   [850]
a cleaving a cutting a splitting a
chopping in two

CHORUS   Where does it come from this godawful
panic,
this rash hysteric-

al clang of your prophetic voice rushing
    over the edge?

KASSANDRA   O marriage of Paris so deadly for everyone
    else
    O river of home my Skamander
      I used to dream by your waters
        now soon enough
    back and forth on the banks of the river of
    hell
      I will walk with my song torn open   [860]

CHORUS   Why are you suddenly speaking clear as day?
    A newborn child could construe what you
    say.
    It gives me a bloody pain
    to hear all the griefs you name.

KASSANDRA   [scream] [scream] [scream] for my ruined city
      [scream] for the offerings my father made
          to save its towers he
      killed animal after animal
       it did no good
        we suffered anyway   [870]
          and I am soon to hit the ground
    I with my *thermonous*
      thermonous means hot soul, burning mind,
      brain on fire

CHORUS   You're back on track.
    Some heavy spirit swoops on you and takes
    your breath—

out comes Death.
(Outcomes? I'm not sure
    where this will end.)

KASSANDRA   Okay. No longer.
No longer now out from veils like some
    firstblush bride
shall my oracle glance   [880]
but as brightness blows the rising sun open
it will rush my oceans forward onto light—
a wave of woes far worse than these.
No more riddles.
Bear me witness:
I know that smell. Evils. Evils long ago.
A chorus of singers broods upon this house,
    they never leave,
their tune is bad, they drink cocktails of
    human blood and party through the
    rooms.
You will not get them out.
They are kin to the Furies and sing of
    original evil,   [890]
marriage beds that stink of life gone wrong.
Do I miss the mark? Am I a prophet of lies?
    Just babbling?
Or do you admit I'm a pretty good shot.
Bear me witness:
I see this place I see its ancient sins.

CHORUS   You amaze me. It's as if you were born here.

KASSANDRA   You can thank Apollo.

CHORUS   He desired you?

KASSANDRA   I was ashamed to speak of it before.

CHORUS   Let's not be overdelicate.   [900]

KASSANDRA   The fact is we wrestled.

CHORUS   Had sex?

KASSANDRA   I said yes but defaulted.

CHORUS   And you already possessed your gift?

KASSANDRA   My gift. Oh yes. I was the local prophet.

CHORUS   So did Apollo punish you?

KASSANDRA   He made my prophecy never believed.

CHORUS   But we believed y—

KASSANDRA   *[scream]* I lose my screams they find me
                again!
            The dread work of prophecy buckles me
                down to its BAM BAM BAM—   [910]
            do you see them there those young ones
                who nest by the door
            like shapes in dreams
            like children murdered
            they hold their own flesh in their own
                hands

and the entrails drip where their father
    tasted deep.
Yes I can see this and I tell you vengeance is
    coming—
a soft lion tumbles in the master's bed
awaiting him—
how little the great general understands
that bitch who licked his hand at the door
    of the house   [920]
and what she plans to do.
She has the nerve, she is a killer, female
    against male.
What should I call her—a kind of snake, a
    Skylla, a plague, a mother who breathes
    out
war against her own loved ones?
How she shrieked in joy
to see that man on her doorstep.
Yet you know it's all the same to me if
    anyone believes this or not.
Who cares? The future is coming.
Soon enough you'll pity me,
you'll say I was a true prophet.   [930]

CHORUS   Thyestes feasting on his children's flesh—
    I get that one, it makes me cold with fear.
    After that you were unclear.

KASSANDRA   I say you will see Agamemnon dead.

CHORUS   Hush, girl.

KASSANDRA   There is no hushing this.

CHORUS   Really? Really? I pray you are wrong!

KASSANDRA   Pray away. *They* are preparing to kill.

CHORUS   They? Who? What man do you mean?

KASSANDRA   You haven't been listening at all have you?   [940]

CHORUS   Just tell me what he's planning to do.

KASSANDRA   And yet I speak Greek all too well.

CHORUS   So do the Pythian oracles but no one
      understands them.

KASSANDRA   *[scream]* Again! The fire comes on me.
      [scream] For Apollo! *[scream]* For me!
   Look there—see the lioness who beds a
      wolf when the lion is gone?
   She'll kill me, she's mixing a cup of anger
      and death even now,
   she's whetting her sword on her husband's
      head—
   she'll make him pay for bringing me home!
   So why do I keep this ridiculous costume,
      these "prophetic symbols" the stick the
      crown—
   be gone! be damned! Enrich someone else's
      life with doom!   [950]

Look, Apollo himself is denuding me—
he watched them mock me in my little
    prophet's dress, my little prophet's hat.
They called me *gypsy beggar starveling*, I put
    up with that.
And now the prophet forces his prophetess
    down to the killing floor.
Instead of my father's altar a butcher's block
    awaits me
and a hot rip of blood.
I am meat for sacrifice.
But I won't go unavenged.
Another is coming, a son to kill the mother
    and pay the father's debt—
strangered from this land he will go into
    exile   [960]
then come back one day to finish it off.
The gods have sworn an oath on this.
So why call for pity?
I saw Troy fall. I see Troy's victors falling.
Now I go to die. *Hello gates of Hades.*
I pray for an easy death: one clean stroke
    and then—
I close my eyes.

CHORUS   That was a long speech. But your wisdom
    does not falter.
On the other hand, if you know you have
    an appointment with death
why stride so calmly to the altar?   [970]

KASSANDRA   There is no escape.

CHORUS　No, you still have time.

KASSANDRA　The day is come. Flight would be pointless.

CHORUS　Brave girl.

KASSANDRA　People never say that to a lucky person do
　　　　they?

CHORUS　What about the glamour of a noble death?

KASSANDRA　Alas for my glamorous father and his noble
　　　　children.

CHORUS　What's the matter? Why do you jump back?

KASSANDRA　*[scream] [scream]*

CHORUS　Why do you scream? You seem suddenly
　　　　disgusted.　　　　　　　　　　　　　　[980]

KASSANDRA　The house is reeking blood!

CHORUS　Well yes, they're sacrificing animals at the
　　　　hearth.

KASSANDRA　I know that smell! It isn't animals!

CHORUS　Incense maybe?

KASSANDRA　Here I go. To raise a funeral song for me
　　　　and Agamemnon.

My life is over.
Oh my friends, I'm not making a fuss
   like a bird at a bush—
you can testify to that after I'm dead.
I speak as one about to die:
there will be other deaths in consequence of
   me, a woman then a man.   [990]
Remember what I was.

CHORUS   How I pity you and your death foretold.

KASSANDRA   One thing left.
I want to sing my own dirge.
I pray to the sun, to this last minute of life:
let my enemies pay with blood for what
   they did to me—
I'm just a killed slave, easy fistful of death.
But you,
      O humans,
              O human things—   [1000]
when a man is happy, a shadow could
   overturn it.
When life goes wrong, a wet sponge erases
   the whole picture.
You,
     you,
        I pity.

[Exit KASSANDRA.*]*

CHORUS   No human ever has enough good fortune.
No one ever bars it from his door.

Agamemnon won from gods the right to
    capture Priam's city.
If he must shed his blood to pay for others
    in the past
and then by dying pass the debt to others in
    the future,   [1010]
who in the world can say that he is safe?

[Cry from within.]

AGAMEMNON   *[scream]* I am struck!

CHORUS   Silence! Who cries out?

AGAMEMNON   *[scream]* Again! I am hit a second time!

CHORUS   *[severally]* —Those screams imply the deed is
    done but let's go slow.
    —My advice is summon the townsfolk
    here.
    —I say burst in and catch them unaware.
    —Something like that, something like that,
    I agree.
    —It's obvious they're laying the ground for
    tyranny.
    —And we're wasting time while they defy
    the goddess named Delay.   [1020]
    —Oh I don't know what to do or what to
    think or what to say.
    —Me neither. Words can't raise the dead.
    —Do you want those criminals down on
    your head?

—Unendurable. Death is better.

—So from two screams we're saying the
      king's a dead letter?

—Well let's not get upset till we clarify this
      thing.

—That's my vote. Find out what's going on
      with our king.

[Dead bodies of AGAMEMNON *and* KASSANDRA
are displayed on the stage with KLYTAIMESTRA
standing over them.]

KLYTAIMESTRA   I said a lot of things before that sounded
                           nice.

I'm not ashamed to contradict them now.

How else devise damage for an enemy who
      passed himself off as a friend?   [1030]

How else fence up nets high enough to
      catch him?

It's a long long time I've been pondering
      this.

Crisis of an ancient feud.

Finally, I say finally!

I stand where I struck with the deed done!

I did it. I make no denial.

So he could neither flee nor save himself

I threw round him a cloth with no way
      out—a sort of dragnet—

evil wealth of cloth.

I strike him twice.   [1040]

Two screams and his limbs go slack.

He falls. I strike him one more time—three
    for Zeus the savior of corpses!
And as he sputters out his life in blood
he sprays me with black drops like dew
gladdening me no less than when the green
    buds of the corn feel showers from
    heaven!
That's how things stand, old men of Argos.
Rejoice if you want to. I am on top
    of the world!
And this man has the libation he deserves.
He filled this house like a mixing bowl
    to the brim with evils,
now he has drunk it down.   [1050]

CHORUS   Your mouth is amazing.
Who would boast like this over a husband?

KLYTAIMESTRA   Don't squawk at me. I'm not some witless
    female.
I am fearless and you know it.
Whether you praise or blame me I don't
    care.
Here lies Agamemnon, my husband, a dead
    body, work of my righteous right hand.
That's how things stand.

CHORUS   What poison did you eat or drink to make
    you so insane?
You've cast off, cut off, everything—you
    will be cityless,

accursed,   [1060]
an object of hatred,
toxic to your own people.

KLYTAIMESTRA   Oh *now* you pull out your code of justice—
                   call *me* accursed, demand *my* exile!
               What about *them*? What about *him*?
               This man who, without a second thought,
                   as if it were a goat dying,
               sacrificed his own child,
               my most beloved, my birthpang, my own—
                   and he had flocks of animals
               to charm the winds of Thrace!
               Isn't it this man you should have sent into
                   exile, to pay for that polluted deed?
               Instead you pass judgment on me!   [1070]
               Well I warn you, threaten me all you like
               and yes, if you crush me, you'll be giving the
                   orders.
               But if some god ordains the opposite,
               however late, old men, I'll teach you
                   your place.

CHORUS   You swaggering egotist.
               Your mind is mad with killing.
               I see a stain of blood upon your eye.
               But you know one day when you've lost
                   both friends and honor,
               you'll have to repay blow for blow.

KLYTAIMESTRA   Listen and keep listening: this I swear to
                   you.   [1080]

By the Justice of my child, by Ruin, by
   Revenge—
the three gods for whom I slaughtered
   him—
hope does not walk the halls of fear in me
so long as Aigisthos lights the fire on my
   hearth.
Aigisthos is loyal. A good defender.
   My personal shield.
Here lies the man who despoiled me,
   darling of every fancy girl at Troy.
And by his side the little prophetess who
   sweetened his sheets.
Sweetened the whole army's sheets, I
   shouldn't doubt.
They got what they deserve those two.
Yes here he lies. And she like a swan that has
   sung its last song   [1090]
beside him, his truelove, his little
   spiceberry.
You know, to look at them
   kind of excites me.

CHORUS   How I wish that I could fall asleep and not
                wake up.
        Our guardian is gone, the gracious man
                 who
             for a woman's sake
            suffered so much and
            by a woman's hand
            is now cut down.

Helen! wild mad Helen,
you murdered so many beneath Troy.   [1100]
Now you've crowned yourself one final
perfect time,
a crown of blood that will not wash away.
Strife walks with you everywhere you go.

KLYTAIMESTRA   Oh stop whining.
And why get angry at Helen?
As if she singlehandedly destroyed those
multitudes of men.
As if she all alone
made this wound in us.

CHORUS   I call upon the evil demon who besets this
house,
who besets the sons of Tantalos,   [1110]
you whose power comes from women,
whose voice is like a crow,
you perch upon the corpse
harshing out your hymn of joy!

KLYTAIMESTRA   Now you're making sense—
to call upon the thricegorged evil demon of
this family.
Deep in its nerves is a lust to lick blood
and no wound heals
before the next starts oozing.

CHORUS   This demon you admire sits heavy on the
house,   [1120]
heavy with anger,

a ruinous insatiable thing.
[scream] For the sake of Zeus!
Zeus is the cause,
Zeus is the action.
Whatever happens for mortals without
Zeus?
What part of all this is not
godaccomplished?

O how shall I lament you O my king?
My heart is full of love.
But you lie in this spider's web leaking out
your life—   [1130]
a death unholy, a bed unworthy,
a blade coming out of your own wife's
hand.

KLYTAIMESTRA   You call this deed mine?
And I his wife? You're wrong!
Some ancient bitter spirit of revenge
disguised as Agamemnon's wife
arose from Atreus' brutal feast
to sacrifice this man for those little children.

CHORUS   You are guiltless of this murder?
Who is your witness? I don't think so!   [1140]
Oh yes, some spirit of vengeance may have
been your secret sharer.
Ares is black with wading through blood
and he will get justice
for the clotted gore of children used as food.

O how shall I lament you O my king?
My heart is full of love.
But you lie in this spider's web leaking out
your life—
a death unholy, a bed unworthy,
a blade coming out of your own wife's
hand.   [1150]

KLYTAIMESTRA   His death was nothing unworthy!
Did he not bring lies and ruin on this
house?
My poor little green shoot Iphigeneia—
she's the one
who suffered unworthy.
He has nothing to complain about.
He paid by the sword for what he himself
began.

CHORUS   I am at a loss. I have no idea
where to turn, everything's falling apart.
A storm of blood beats on the roof—no
more little drops!
I'm terrified.   [1160]
Justice is sharpening
a second sword
on a second whetstone.

O earth I wish you had wrapt me away
before I saw my king sprawled in a bath!
Who will bury him? Who will mourn
him—*you*?

You'd have the nerve to sing his lament
as if you were doing him a favor?
Who in the world will shed true tears at this
man's tomb?

KLYTAIMESTRA   That's not your concern.   [1170]
By me he fell, by me he died, I shall bury
him.
Not with wailing from this house.
No, Iphigeneia will open her arms
and run to meet him in Hades—
a father-daughter embrace,
won't that be perfect!

CHORUS   She shoots back taunt for taunt.
How to judge? The thief is robbed, the
killer pays his price.
But here's the key: while Zeus sits on his
throne
the doer must suffer. That is the law.   [1180]
Who could drive the curse out of this
family?
These people are glued to ruin.

KLYTAIMESTRA   Well, that's a good point.
But I for one propose to swear a truce with
the demon of this house.
I'll be content with where we've got to
now,
hard though it is to bear.
Let the demon go grind out murders on
some other family.

I'm happy with a tiny share of the wealth
here
if I can stop us all killing one another.

[Enter AIGISTHOS.]

AIGISTHOS   O welcome day of justice! Now I can say
the gods are handling miscreants as they
should,   [1190]
when I see this fellow lying in robes that the
Furies wove—
it's payback for his father's crimes.
I am oh! quite pleased.
For Atreus you know, who was ruler of this
land and this man's father,
drove Thyestes, who was my father and this
man's brother—am I making myself
clear?—
out of his city and away from his home.
Then when he (Thyestes) returned as a
suppliant to his (Atreus') hearth
Atreus set before my dad, with hospitality
more zealous than kind,
a merry meal of his own children's flesh.
The toes and fingers he chopped up
especially small.   [1200]
Thyestes took a chunk and ate it, not
knowing.
That meal ruined our family, as you can see.
He suddenly saw what he'd done, shrieked
aloud, fell back

vomiting carnage and called out a curse
    upon this house,
kicking over the table to emphasize it:
May the entire race of Pelops perish this same
    way!
So that's why you see this man lying here
    dead.
I planned it. Righteously.
For he exiled me too, along with my poor
    father, when I was quite young.
Justice brought me back.   [1210]
From exile I laid my finger on this man,
    devising every detail of his doom.
And you know, even death would be sweet
    to me now
I've seen him caught in the nets of Justice.

CHORUS   Aigisthos, your roostering repels me.
You say you intended to kill this man,
    plotted his pitiful murder all alone.
And I say you're a candidate for stoning.
    Know it.
The people will bring you to justice.

AIGISTHOS   Don't squawk at me from your seat on the
    lowest rowing bench:
I run this ship. Know it.
You may be old but you'll learn to control
    your impulses.   [1220]
Bondage and hunger are wonderful
    teachers.

Have you eyes? Don't you see? If you kick
    against the pricks,
you'll hurt yourself.

CHORUS   *Woman!* You skulk at home while men are
    off at war.
You foul the bed of our king and plot his
    death!

AIGISTHOS   You'll be sorry you said that.
You're the opposite of Orpheus, whose
    voice could charm.
Your silly yelping infuriates me.
But you will be rendered acquiescent.

CHORUS   As if *you* could ever be my master—you
    who dreamed of a king's murder   [1230]
but had not the nerve to do the deed
    yourself!

AIGISTHOS   Well, no. To entrap him was the wife's work,
    obviously.
An old enemy like me would have been
    instantly suspicious.
But with his wealth I plan to rule this state
    and whomever does not obey me
I'll yoke to a heavy collar. Hunger and
    darkness will break him down.

CHORUS   Given the rot in your soul, why not kill the
    king yourself?

Instead a woman has polluted our land and
    our gods.

Does Orestes somewhere look upon the
    light?

I pray he come back and put you two to
    death!

AIGISTHOS   If that is your attitude, you'll soon learn—   [1240]

CHORUS   Come! Men! There's work to do!

AIGISTHOS   *[To his guards.]* Swords up!

CHORUS   Death, you say! We're ready.

AIGISTHOS   Good, you'll soon taste it.

KLYTAIMESTRA   No, no, no, no, my dear darling, no more
    evil.

The harvest is in: we have enough pain,
    enough bloodshed.

Venerable elders, go back to your homes,
    before you suffer.

What we did

had to be done.

And if it ends here, we're content.   [1250]

Some demon of luck has clipped us
    with a sharp hoof.

That's a woman's opinion, for what it's
    worth.

AIGISTHOS   You mean these creatures are permitted to
                    pelt me with insults
              heedlessly, randomly, treating it like a game?

CHORUS   You won't see men of Argos cringe
                    before a coward!

AIGISTHOS   I'll come after you!

CHORUS   Not if the gods bring Orestes back!

AIGISTHOS   Empty hope! The food of exiles!

CHORUS   Go on, be yourself, grow fat, pollute justice,
                    now is your chance!

AIGISTHOS   One day you'll pay.   [1260]

CHORUS   Brag away! You're like a cock beside his hen.

KLYTAIMESTRA Ignore their yelpings.
              You and I, as masters of this house, will
                    dispose all things as they should be.
              Beautifully.

              [Exeunt.]

ELEKTRA

by Sophokles

INTRODUCTION

HER

Her name sounds like a negative adjective: "alektra" in Greek means "bedless, unwed, unmarriageable." Her life is a stopped and stranded thing, just a glitch in other people's plans. Her function and meaning as a human have been reduced to one activity—saying *no* to everything around her. *No* to her father's murder at the hands of her mother, *no* to her mother's adultery with Aigisthos, *no* to going on with her life as if nothing were wrong, *no* to breaking off her lament.

People sometimes say of Elektra that her mourning is excessive. She would not disagree. Early in the play she confesses to the chorus:

> *Women, I am ashamed before you: I know*
> *you find me extreme*
> *in my grief.*
> *I bear it hard.*
> *But I tell you I have no choice.*
> *(338–42)*

She has no choice, because she has no other self than the one that mourns. She is clear about this:

I cannot not grieve.

(181)

Locked between the two negatives of this despairing sentence is the whole range of her options as Elektra. Again her clarity:

I need one food:
I must not violate Elektra.
(494–95)

What does it mean to "not violate Elektra"? Her sense of self is amazing. Pressure comes from every side, from everyone around her, to acquiesce in the crimes of her mother and keep outrage quiet. Pressure has partly succeeded: she is deformed. Psychologically and morally she has no room to breathe or move. And she knows this. She says to the chorus:

Evil is a pressure that shapes us to itself.
(424)

Later, more bitterly, to her mother:

I am the shape you made me.
Filth teaches filth.
(836–37)

To "violate Elektra" would be to stop saying *no* to evil and filth. Sophokles is a playwright fascinated in general by people who say *no*, people who resist compromise, people who make stumbling blocks of themselves, like Antigone or Ajax. These characters usually express defiance in some heroic action—Antigone buries her brother, Ajax falls on his sword. Elektra has the same kind of raw, stubborn, scandalous soul, but her circumstances are different: Elektra is deprived of action.

The play begins with two men center stage making a plan that will change her life and deciding not to tell her about it, although she is hovering just inside the door (they hear her weeping). The play ends with two men center stage marching into the house to complete the revenge plot while Elektra is left outside to follow after them or stand and wait, no one seems to care. The play's centerpiece is a deception scene in which two men manipulate Elektra with lies to a point of near hysteria. She is an adult but unmarried female in the house of a mother who hates her and she has neither social function nor emotional context. She seems to squat on the doorstep of the house rather than live inside. Her sister calls her a maniac and waves her ideas away. Her brother treats her as superfluous to his plans—he finds her wild, emotional, depressing. She is a woman stranded at doorways and passivity is killing her.

There is only one thing she can do.

Make noise.

So Elektra talks, wails, argues, denounces, sings, chants and screams from one end of the play to the other. She is onstage almost every minute and has one of the longest speaking parts in Greek tragedy. Sounds of every kind emerge from her, articulate and inarticulate. Her power of language is fantastic; she can outtalk anyone in the play. Her vocabulary of screams is so rich that I chose to transliterate her cries letter for letter—OIMOI! instead of the conventional *Alas!* or *Woe is me!*[1] This is not a person who would say *Woe is me!* She is a torrent of self. Actionless, yet she causes things to happen and people to change. Hopeless, yet she keeps Elektra going. There are moments when she transcends herself in words, as in her opening prayer to light and air:

---

1. I have written about this elsewhere: see "Screaming in Translation," in Peter Burian and Alan Shapiro, eds., *Sophocles: Electra* (New York: Oxford University Press, 2001), 41–48.

> *O holy light!*
> *And equal air shaped on the world—*
> *(116)*

There are moments that condense her to pure hate, as when she hurls at her mother:

> *Call me*
> *baseminded, blackmouthing bitch! if you like—*
> *for if this is my nature*
> *we know how I come by it, don't we?*
> *(815–18)*

She is no Antigone—not noble or lovable or "deserving of golden honor," as Sophokles says of that other lone female. But she is always worth listening to.

PLAY

Overall it is "a play without comfort," as Fiona Shaw said when she undertook the part of Elektra.[2] In particular she found the deception/recognition scene between Elektra and Orestes "unspeakably impossible to play." Critics and scholars (and translators) agree, this scene is a hard nut to crack. Why does Orestes decide to trick his sister into thinking he's dead? Why does he give it up in the middle? What does Sophokles want to achieve here? The alternation of lies and truth, high emotions and low, is bewildering and cruel, the tug-of-war over an empty urn almost bizarre. Fiona Shaw describes it this way:

2. The production was directed by Deborah Warner and played in London, Paris, Bradford, Glasgow and Derry in the early 1990s. See Fiona Shaw, "Electra Speechless," in Francis M. Dunn, ed., *Sophocles' Electra in Performance* (Stuttgart, 2001), 131–38.

To have decided your brother is dead and then to hear he's alive and
then to hear he's dead again and then to hear he's alive again scrambles
the brain. There cannot be any recovery from it . . . It's like playing a
very low note and suddenly playing a very high note and you break
the voice on the way. You break everything.[3]

Despite its difficulty, she says the scene proved exceptionally
moving in performance. Audiences wept. Audiences also wept in
the fourth century B.C. when the celebrated actor Polos played
the part. According to ancient gossip, Polos had only recently lost
by death a beloved son when he was invited to do Sophokles'
Elektra in a revival of it at Athens. This was his approach:

Having costumed himself in the mourning garb of Elektra, Polos took
from the tomb the ashes and urn of his son, embraced them as if they
were those of Orestes and filled the whole place not with the
appearance and imitation of sorrow but with genuine grief and
unfeigned lamentation. It seemed the play was being acted but this was
in fact real heartbreak.[4]

This story is probably just a story. But it gives me pause, I
think because it draws out a strand of uneasiness that is already
present in Sophokles' construction of the scene. I mean his play
with fakery. For isn't it deeply odd that Elektra's profoundest
emotional outpouring, the lament for Orestes during which
"you break everything," as Fiona Shaw says, should be evoked
by a fake object—this funeral urn that is supposed to contain
Orestes' ashes but in fact contains nothing? What does "in fact"
mean in such a context? The "fact" that Polos is exploiting and

3. Ibid., 136.
4. Aulus Gellius, *Attic Nights* 6.5, vol. 2 (Cambridge: Harvard University Press,
1927), 35–37.

the "fact" that Sophokles is staging are facts of different orders, yet they fit one within the other within theatrical experience. Sophokles may have constructed the urn scene to question this fit. I doubt he would have approved Polos using his own son's death to get a strong performance, but he seems (in other plays as well as *Elektra*) very alert to the boundary between art and reality and sometimes inclined to fiddle with it himself.[5]

To look at the matter from another angle: Could the recognition scene have been staged differently? We have a good example. Orestes' story is a standard myth told and retold by poets from Homer to Euripides. But Sophokles' closest model was probably *Choephoroi* (*Libation Bearers*), the second play of Aiskhylos' *Oresteia*, staged in 458 B.C.: here we see a recognition scene between brother and sister that it is straightforwardly joyful—no deception of Elektra, no tormenting her with a fake funeral urn, no ironic byplay. Emotions run easy and true to their goal, vengeance seems justified in the eyes of (at least some of) the gods, and two murderous children are (arguably) redeemed by mutual love. In Sophokles' replay, all this is displaced and estranged. He subtracts redemption and leaves justice vague. Focus is on Elektra—shattered and elated, manipulated and suppressed by turns, her poor soul subject to someone else's script, her responses coerced by their staging. "You have used me strangely," she says to Orestes finally (1754).

We can say for pretty sure that Sophokles was thinking of Aiskhylos when he composed his *Elektra*, because he quotes him. The death scene of Klytaimestra in Sophokles' play echoes the death scene of Agamemnon in Aiskhylos' *Agamemnon*, even down

---

5. See Mark Ringer, *Elektra and the Empty Urn: Metatheater and Role Playing in Sophocles* (Chapel Hill: University of North Carolina Press, 1998), and further bibliography there.

to reiterating the death cries that emerge from the house in each case. Elektra's horrific command to Orestes

Hit her a second time, if you have the strength!
(Sophokles' Elektra 1885)

is a direct quotation of her father's pitiful

Again! I am hit a second time!
(Aiskhylos' Agamemnon 1014)

It's as if the whole family were there, knee-deep in blood, and Elektra is killing her mother with her father's words. Why would Sophokles do this? To emphasize Elektra's awful command of language as a weapon? To remind us of Klytaimestra's crime and close the cycle of vengeance in this house? To reopen Agamemnon's wounds and suggest that vengeance here will never end? To trump Aiskhylos? To pay homage to Aiskhylos?[6] Perhaps all these at once. Sophokles is a complex poet working in a complex tradition. His audience enjoys all kinds of play with masks. All kinds of uses of urns. They do not come to the theater for comfort.

---

6. "Every poem is a misinterpretation of a parent poem," says Harold Bloom in *The Anxiety of Influence* (New York: Oxford University Press, 1977). Bloom doesn't quite believe in homage.

DRAMATIS PERSONAE

(in order of appearance)

OLD MAN	*servant and former tutor of Orestes*
ORESTES	*son of Klytaimestra and Agamemnon*
CHRYSOTHEMIS	*daughter of Klytaimestra and Agamemnon*
ELEKTRA	*daughter of Klytaimestra and Agamemnon*
KLYTAIMESTRA	*queen of Argos*
AIGISTHOS	*paramour of Klytaimestra*
CHORUS	*of Mykenaian women*
PYLADES	*Orestes' silent friend*

SETTING: *Before the palace of Agamemnon in Argos.*

[Enter the OLD MAN *and* ORESTES *with* PYLADES.*]*

OLD MAN   You are his son! Your father
             marshaled the armies at Troy once—
             . child of Agamemnon: look around you now.
             Here is the land you were longing to see all
                 that time.
             Ancient Argos. You dreamed of this place.
             The grove of Io, where the gadfly drove her.
             Look, Orestes. There is the marketplace
             named for Apollo,
             wolfkiller god.   [10]
             And on the left, the famous temple of Hera.
             But stop! There—do you know what that is?
             Mykenai. Yes. Look at it. Walls of gold!
             Walls of death. It is the house of Pelops.
             I got you out of there
             out of the midst of your father's murder,
             one day long ago.
             From the hands of your sister
             I carried you off. Saved your life. Reared
                 you up—
             to this: to manhood. To avenge your father's
                 death.

So, Orestes! And you, dear   [20]
Pylades—
Now is the time to decide what to do.
Already the sun is hot upon us.
Birds are shaking, the world is awake.
Black stars and night have died away.
So before anyone is up and about
let's talk.
Now is no time to delay.
This is the edge of action.

ORESTES   I love you, old man.   [30]
The signs of goodness shine from your face.
Like a thoroughbred horse—he gets old,
but he does not lose heart,
he pricks up his ears—so you
urge me forward
and stand in the front rank yourself.
Good. Now,
I will outline my plan. You
listen sharp.
If I'm off target anywhere,   [40]
set me straight.
You see, I went to Pytho
to ask the oracle how I could get justice
from the killers of my father.
Apollo answered:

Take no weapons.
No shield.
No army.

Go alone—a hand in the night.
Snare them.   [50]
Slaughter them.
You have the right.

That is the oracle.
Here is the plan:
you go into the house at the first chance.
Find out all that is happening there.
Find out and report to us. Be very clear.
You're so old, they won't know you.
And your garlands will fool them.
Now this is your story: [60]
you're a stranger from Phokis,
from the house of Phanoteus
(he's the most powerful ally they have).
Tell them on oath that Orestes is dead.
An accident. Fatal:
rolled out of his chariot on the racetrack at
    Delphi.
Dragged to death under the wheels.
Let that be the story.
Meanwhile, we go to my father's grave,
as Apollo commanded,   [70]
to pour libation and crown the tomb
with locks of hair cut from my head.
Then we'll be back
with that bronzeplated urn
(you know, the one I hid in the bushes).
Oh yes, we'll fool them
with this tale of me dead,

burnt,
nothing left but ash.
What good news for them!   [80]

As for me—
what harm can it do
to die in words?
I save my life and win glory besides!
Can a mere story be evil? No,
   of course not—
so long as it pays in the end.
I know of shrewd men
who die a false death
so as to come home
all the more valued.   [90]
Yes, I am sure:
I will stand clear of this lie
and break on my enemies like a star.

O land of my fathers! O gods of this place!
Take me in. Give me luck on this road.
House of my father:
I come to cleanse you with justice.
I come sent by gods.
Do not exile me from honor!
Put me in full command   [100]
of the wealth and the house!
Enough talk.
Old man, look to your task.
We are off.
This is the point on which everything hinges.
This is the moment of proof.

ELEKTRA   *[A cry from inside the house.]* IO MOI MOI
          DYSTENOS.

OLD MAN   What was that? I heard
          a cry—some servant in the house?

ORESTES   Can it be poor Elektra?   [110]
          Should we stay here and listen?

OLD MAN   No. Nothing precedes the work of Apollo.
          That is our first step: your father's libations.
          That is the way to win: action.

          [Exit the OLD MAN *and* ORESTES *with*
          PYLADES. *Enter* ELEKTRA *from the palace.]*

ELEKTRA   O holy light!
          And equal air shaped on the world—
          you hear my songs,
          you hear the blows fall.
          You know the blood runs
          when night sinks away.   [120]
          All night I watch.
          All night I mourn,
          in this bed that I hate in this house I
              detest.
          How many times can a heart break?
          Oh Father,
          it was not killer Ares
          who opened his arms
          in some foreign land
          to welcome you.

But my own mother and her lover
    Aigisthos: [130]
those two good woodsmen
took an axe and split you down like an oak.
No pity for these things,
there is no pity
but mine,
oh Father,
for the pity of your butchering rawblood
    death.

Never
will I leave off lamenting,
never. No.   [140]
As long as the stars sweep through heaven.
As long as I look on this daylight.
No.
Like the nightingale who lost her child
I will stand in his doorway
and call on his name.
Make them all hear.
Make this house echo.
O Hades!
Persephone!   [150]
Hermes of hell!
Furies, I call you!
Who watch
when lives are murdered.
Who watch when loves betray.
Come! Help me! Strike back!
Strike back for my father murdered!
And send my brother to me.

Because
alone,   [160]
the whole poised force of my life is nothing
against this.

[Enter CHORUS.*]*

CHORUS   Your mother is evil
but oh my child why
melt your life away in mourning?
Why let grief eat you alive?
It was long ago
she took your father:
her hand came out of unholy dark
and cut him down.   [170]
I curse the one
who did the deed
(if this is right to say).

ELEKTRA   You are women of noble instinct
and you come to console me
in my pain.
I know.
I do understand.
But I will not let go this man or this
           mourning.

He is my father.   [180]
I cannot not grieve.
Oh my friends,
Friendship is a tension. It makes delicate
           demands.

I ask this one thing:
let me go mad in my own way.

CHORUS   Not from Hades' black and universal lake
           can you lift him.
         not by groaning, not by prayers.
         Yet you run yourself out
         in a grief with no cure,
         no time limit, no measure.   [190]
         It is a knot no one can untie.
         Why are you so in love with
         things unbearable?

ELEKTRA None but a fool or an infant
         could forget a father
         gone so far and cold.
         No.
         Lament is a pattern cut and fitted around
           my mind—
         like the bird who calls Itys! Itys! endlessly,
         bird of grief,   [200]
         angel of Zeus.
         O heartdragging Niobe,
         I count you a god:
         buried in rock yet
         always you weep.

CHORUS   You are not the only one in the world,
         my child, who has stood in the glare of
           grief.
         Compare yourself:
         you go too far.

Look at your sister, Chrysothemis: [210]
she goes on living. So does Iphianassa.
And the boy—his secret years are sorrowful
     too,
but he will be brilliant
one day when Mykenai welcomes him
     home
to his father's place, to his own land
in the guidance of Zeus—
Orestes!

ELEKTRA   Him yes!
I am past exhaustion
in waiting for him—   [220]
no children,
no marriage,
no light in my heart.
I live in a place of tears.
And he
simply forgets.
Forgets what he suffered,
forgets what he knew.
Messages reach me, each one belied.
He is passionate—as any lover.   [230]
But his passion does not bring him here.

CHORUS   Have courage,
my child.
Zeus is still great in heaven,
he watches and governs all things.
Leave this anger to Zeus: it burns too high
     in you.

Don't hate so much.
Nor let memory go.
For time is a god who can simplify all.
And as for Orestes   [240]
on the shore of Krisa
where oxen graze—
he does not forget you.
Nor is the king of death
on the banks of Acheron
unaware.

ELEKTRA   But meanwhile most of my life has slid by
without hope.
I sink.
I melt.   [250]
Father has gone and there is no man left
who cares enough to stand up for me.
Like some beggar
wandered in off the street,
I serve as a slave
in the halls of my father.
Dressed in these rags,
I stand at the table
and feast on air.

CHORUS   One rawblood cry   [260]
on the day he returned,
one rawblood cry went through the halls
just as the axeblade
rose
and fell.
He was caught by guile,

cut down by lust:
together they bred a thing shaped
   like a monster—
god or mortal
no one knows.   [270]

ELEKTRA   That day tore out the nerves of my life.
That night:
far too silent the feasting,
much too sudden
the silence.
My father looked up and saw
death coming out of their hands.
Those hands took my life hostage.
Those hands murdered me.
I pray   [280]
the great god of Olympos
give them pain on pain to pay for this!
And smother the glow
of deeds like these.

CHORUS   Think again, Elektra.
Don't say any more.
Don't you see what you're doing?
You make your own pain.
Why keep wounding yourself?
With so much evil stored up   [290]
in that cold dark soul of yours

you breed enemies everywhere you touch.
But you must not
clash with the people in power.

ELEKTRA   By dread things I am compelled. I know
              that.
           I see the trap closing.
           I know what I am.
           But while life is in me
           I will not stop this violence. No.
           Oh my friends   [300]
           who is there to comfort me?
           Who understands?
           Leave me be,
           let me go,
           do not soothe me.
           This is a knot no one can untie.
           There will be no rest,
           there is no retrieval.
           No number exists for
           griefs like these.   [310]

CHORUS   Yes but I speak from concern—
           as a mother would: trust me.
           Do not breed violence out of violence.

ELEKTRA   All right then, you tell me one thing—
           at what point does the evil level off in my
              life?
           You say ignore the deed—is that right?
           Who could approve this?
           It defies human instinct!
           Such ethics make no sense to me.
           And how could I nestle myself
              in a life of ease   [320]

while my father lies out in the cold,
outside honor?
My cries are wings:
they pierce the cage.
For if a dead man is earth and nothing,
if a dead man is void and dead space lying,
if a dead man's murderers
do not give
blood for blood
to pay for this,   [330]
then shame does not exist.
Human reverence
is gone.

CHORUS   I came here, child, because I care
          for your welfare as my own.
          But perhaps I am wrong.
          Let it be as you say.

ELEKTRA   Women, I am ashamed before you: I know
          you find me extreme
          in my grief.   [340]
          I bear it hard.
          But I tell you I have no choice.
          It compels. I act because it compels.
          Oh forgive me. But how could I—
          how could a woman of any nobility
          stand
          and watch her father's house go bad?
          There is something bad here,
          growing. Day and night
          I watch it. Growing.   [350]

My mother is where it begins.
She and I are at war.
Our relation is hatred.
And I live in this house
with my father's own killers:
they rule me. They dole out my life.
What kind of days do you think I have
   here?
I see my father's throne
with Aigisthos on it.
I see my father's robes   [360]
with Aigisthos in them.
I see my father's hearth with Aigisthos
   presiding—
right where he stood when he struck
my father down!
And the final outrage:
the killer tucked in my father's bed.
Behold the man who pleasures my mother—
should I call that thing "mother" that lies at
   his side?
God! Her nerve astounds me.
She lives with that polluted object,   [370]
fearing no fury. No,
she laughs!
Celebrates
that day—the day she took my father
with dances and song and slaughter of
   sheep!
A monthly bloodgift to the gods who keep
   her safe.

I watch
all going dark in the rooms of my house.
I weep.
I melt.   [380]
I grieve
for the strange cruel feast made in my
      father's name.
But I grieve to myself:
not allowed even to shed
      the tears I would.
No—that creature
who calls herself noble
will shriek at me:
"Godcursed! You piece of hatred!
So you've lost your father—is that unique?
No mortal mourns but you?   [390]
Damn you.
May the gods of hell damn you
to groan perpetually there
as you groan
perpetually
here!"
That's her style—
and when she hears someone mention
      Orestes,
then she goes wild,
      comes screaming at me:
"Have I you to thank for this?   [400]
Isn't it your work? Wasn't it you
who stole Orestes out of my hands
and smuggled him away?

You'll pay for it.
I tell you, you will pay."
Howling bitch. And by her side
the brave bridegroom—
this lump of bad meat.
With women only
he makes his war.   [410]

And I wait.
I wait.
I wait
for Orestes.
He will come! He will end this.
But my life is dying out.
He is always on the verge of doing something
then does nothing.
He has worn out all the hopes I had or
    could have.
Oh my friends,   [420]
in times like these,
self-control has no meaning.
Rules of reverence do not apply.
Evil is a pressure that shapes us to itself.

CHORUS   Is Aigisthos at home?

ELEKTRA   No. Do you think I'd be
standing outdoors?
He is gone to the fields.

CHORUS   That gives me courage
to say what I came to say.   [430]

ELEKTRA   What is it you want?

CHORUS   I want to know—your brother—
do you say he is coming? Or has a plan?

ELEKTRA   Yes, he says so. But he says a lot. Does
nothing.

CHORUS   A man who does a great deed may hesitate.

ELEKTRA   Oh? I saved his life without hesitating.

CHORUS   Courage. His nature is good, he will not fail
his kin.

ELEKTRA   That belief is what keeps me alive.

CHORUS   Quiet now. Here is your sister come from
the house,
Chrysothemis, of the same father   [440]
and mother as you.
She has offerings in her hands,
as if for the dead.

[Enter CHRYSOTHEMIS carrying garlands and a
vessel.]

CHRYSOTHEMIS   Here you are again at the doorway, sister,
telling your tale to the world!
When will you learn?
It's pointless. Pure self-indulgence.
Yes, I know how bad things are.

I suffer too—if I had the strength
I would show how I hate them.   [450]
But now is not the right time.
In rough waters, lower the sail, is my theory.
Why pretend to be doing,
unless I can do some real harm?
I wish you would see this.
And yet,
it is true,
justice is not on my side.
Your choice is the right one. On the other
        hand,
if I want to live a free woman,   [460]
there are masters who must be obeyed.

ELEKTRA   You appall me.
Think of the father who sired you! But you
        do not.
All your thought is for her.
These sermons you give me are all learned
from Mother, not a word is your own.
Well it's time for you to make a choice:
quit being "sensible"
or keep your good sense and betray your
        own kin.
Wasn't it you who just said,   [470]
"If I had the strength I would show how I
        hate them"!
Yet here I am doing everything possible
to avenge our father,
and do you help? No!

You try to turn me aside.

Isn't this simply cowardice added to evil?

Instruct me—no! Let me tell you:

What do I stand to gain if I cease my
    lament?

Do I not live? Badly, I know, but I live.

What is more,   [480]

I am a violation to them.

And so, honor the dead—

if any grace exists down there.

Now

you hate them, you say.

But this hate is all words.

In fact, you live with the killers.

And I tell you,

if someone were to give me

all the gifts that make your days delicious,   [490]

I would not bend. No.

You can have your rich table

and life flowing over the cup.

I need one food:

I must not violate Elektra.

As for your status, I couldn't care less.

Nor would you, if you had any self-respect.

You could have been called

child of the noblest men!

Instead they call you mother's girl,   [500]

they think you base.

Your own dead father,

your own loved ones,

you do betray.

CHORUS   No anger I pray.
                There is profit for both
                if you listen to each other.

CHRYSOTHEMIS   Her talk is no surprise to me, ladies.
                I'm used to this.
                And I wouldn't have bothered   [510]
                to speak at all, except—
                for the rumor I heard.
                There is very great evil coming this way,
                something to cut her long laments
                short.

ELEKTRA   Tell me what is the terrible thing?
                If it is worse than my present life,
                I give up.

CHRYSOTHEMIS   I tell what I know:
                they plan,   [520]
                unless you cease from this mourning,
                to send you where you will not see the sun
                     again.
                You'll be singing your songs
                alive
                in a room
                in the ground.
                Think about that.
                And don't blame me when you suffer.
                Too late then.
                Now is the time to start being sensible.   [530]

ELEKTRA   Ah. That is their intention, is it.

CHRYSOTHEMIS   It is. As soon as Aigisthos comes home.

ELEKTRA   May he come soon, then.

CHRYSOTHEMIS   What are you saying?

ELEKTRA   Let him come, if he has his plan ready.

CHRYSOTHEMIS   What do you mean? Are you losing your
            mind?

ELEKTRA   I want to escape from you all.

CHRYSOTHEMIS   Not go on living?

ELEKTRA   Living? Oh yes
            my life is a beautiful thing, is it not.   [540]

CHRYSOTHEMIS   Well it could be, if you got some sense.

ELEKTRA   Don't bother telling me to betray those I
            love.

CHRYSOTHEMIS   I tell you we have masters, we must bend.

ELEKTRA   *You* bend—you go ahead and lick their boots.
            It's not my way.

CHRYSOTHEMIS   Don't ruin your life in sheer stupidity.

ELEKTRA   I will ruin my life, if need be,
            avenging our father.

CHRYSOTHEMIS   But our father, I know, forgives us for this.

ELEKTRA   Cowards' talk.   [550]

CHRYSOTHEMIS   You won't listen to reason at all, will you?

ELEKTRA   No. My mind is my own.

CHRYSOTHEMIS   Well then I'll be on my way.

ELEKTRA   Where are you going? Whose offerings are
those?

CHRYSOTHEMIS   Mother is sending me to Father's tomb,
to pour libation.

ELEKTRA   What? To her mortal enemy?

CHRYSOTHEMIS   To her "murder victim," as you like to say.

ELEKTRA   Whose idea was this?

CHRYSOTHEMIS   It came out of a dream in the night, I
believe.   [560]

ELEKTRA   Gods of my father be with me now!

CHRYSOTHEMIS   You take courage from a nightmare?

ELEKTRA   Tell the dream and I'll answer you.

CHRYSOTHEMIS   There is little to tell.

ELEKTRA   Tell it anyway.
              Little words can mean
              death or life sometimes.

CHRYSOTHEMIS Well the story is
              she dreamed of our father
              and knew him again   [570]
              for he came back into the light.
              Then she saw him take hold of his scepter
              and stick it in the hearth—
              his own scepter from the old days,
              that Aigisthos carries now.
              And from the scepter sprang a branch
              in full climbing leaf
              which cast a shadow over the whole land of
                 Mykenai.
              That is as much as I got
              from one who overheard her   [580]
              telling the dream to the sun.
              More I don't know, except
              fear is her reason for sending me out today.
              So I beg you, by the gods of our family,
              listen to me.
              Don't throw your life away on plain stupidity.
              For if you spurn me now,
              you'll come begging later
              when the trouble starts.

ELEKTRA   Oh dear one, no.   [590]
              You cannot touch this tomb
              with any of those things you have in your
                 hands.

It breaks the law. It would be unholy
to bring that woman's libations
to our father: she is the enemy.
No. Pitch them to the winds
or down a dark hole.
They shall come nowhere near his resting
        place.
But when she dies and goes below,
she will find them waiting.   [600]
Treasure keeps, down there.

God! Her nerve is astounding.
What woman alive would send gifts
to garnish her own murder victim?
And do you imagine
the dead man would welcome such
honors
from the hand of the woman who
        butchered him—
think! To clean her blade she wiped it off on
        his head!
You astonish me—do you really believe   [610]
such gifts will cancel murder?
Throw them away.
Here, instead
cut a lock from your hair
and a lock of mine—meager gifts
but it is all I have.
Take this to him, the hair
and this belt of mine,
though it's nothing elaborate.
Kneel down there and pray to him.   [620]

Pray he come up from the ground
to stand with us against our enemies.
Pray that his son Orestes live
to trample his enemies underfoot.
And someday you and I will go in better
        style than this
to crown his tomb.
But I wonder. You know
I wonder—
suppose he had some part
in sending her these cold unlucky dreams.   [630]

Well, never mind that.
Sister,
do this deed.
Stand up for yourself
and for me and for this man we love
more than anyone else in the world,
this dead man. Your father. My father.

CHORUS   The girl speaks for human reverence.
And you,
if you have any sense, will do what she
        says.   [640]

CHRYSOTHEMIS   I will do it. It is the right thing,
why dispute?
But please, my friends,
I need silence from you.
If my mother finds out,
the attempt will turn bitter for me,
I fear.

[Exit CHRYSOTHEMIS.*]*

CHORUS   Unless I am utterly wrong in my reading of
                          omens
              unless I am out of my mind
              Justice is coming   [650]
              with clear signs before her
              and righteousness in her hands.
              She is coming down on us, child, coming
                          now!
              There is courage
              whispering into me
              when I hear tell of these sweetbreathing
                          dreams.
              He does not forget—
              the one who begot you
              the king of the Greeks.
              She does not forget—   [660]
              the jaw that bit him in two:
              ancient and sharpened on both sides to
                          butcher the meat!

              Vengeance is coming—her hands like an
                          army
              her feet as a host.
              She will come out of hiding
              come scorching down
              on love that is filth
              and beds that are blood
              where marriage should never have
                          happened!
              Conviction   [670]

is strong in me:
visions like these are no innocent sign for
   killers.
I say no omens exist
for mortals to read
from the cold faces of dreams
or from oracles
unless this fragment of death steps into the
   daylight.

O horse race of Pelops,
once long ago
you came in the shape of a wide calamity   [680]
to this land.
And from the time when
Myrtilos pitched and sank in the sea
his solid gold life
sliced off at the roots—
never
since that time
has this house
got itself clear of
rawblood   [690]
butchery.

[Enter KLYTAIMESTRA.*]*

KLYTAIMESTRA   Prowling the streets again, are you?
Of course, with Aigisthos away.
He was always the one
who kept you indoors where you couldn't
   embarrass us.

Now that he's gone you pay no heed to me.
Yet you love to make me the text of your
    lectures:
What an arrogant bitchminded tyrant I am,
a living insult to you and your whole way of
    being!
But do I in fact insult you? No. I merely
    return   [700]
the muck you throw at me.
Father, Father, Father! your perpetual
    excuse—
your father got his death from me. From
    me! That's right!
I make no denial.
It was Justice who took him, not I alone.
And you should have helped if you had any
    conscience.
For this father of yours,
this one you bewail,
this unique Greek,
had the heart to sacrifice your own sister to
    the gods.   [710]

And how was that? Did he have some share
in the pain of her birth? No—I did it
    myself!
Tell me:
Why did he cut her throat? What was the
    reason?
You say for the Argives?
But they had no business to kill what was
    mine.

To save Menelaos?
Then I deserved recompense, wouldn't you
    say?
Did not Menelaos have children himself—
in fact two of them,   [720]
who ought to have died before mine
in all fairness?
Their mother, let's not forget,
was the cause of the whole expedition!
Or was it that Hades conceived some
    peculiar desire
to feast on my children instead?
Or perhaps
that murdering thug your father,
simply overlooked my children
in his tender care for Menelaos'.   [730]
Was that not brutal? Was that not perverse?

I say it was.
No doubt you disagree.
But I tell you one thing, that murdered girl
would speak for me if she had a voice.
Anyway, the deed is done.
I feel no remorse.
You think me degenerate?
Here's my advice:
perfect yourself   [740]
before you blame others.

ELEKTRA   At least you can't say I started it this time;
      these ugly remarks are unprovoked.
      But I want to get a few things clear

about the dead man and my sister as well.
If you allow me.

KLYTAIMESTRA Go ahead, by all means. Begin this way
more often
and we won't need ugly remarks at all, will
we?

ELEKTRA All right then. Yes.
You killed my father, you admit.   [750]
What admission could bring more shame?
Never mind if it was legal or not—did you
care?
Let's talk facts: there was only one reason
you killed him.
You were seduced by that creature you live
with.
Ask Artemis,
goddess of hunters,
why she stopped the winds at Aulis.
No, I'll tell you:
my father one day, so I hear,
was out in the grove of the goddess.   [760]
The sound of his footfall startled a stag out
from cover
and, when he killed it, he let fall a boast.
This angered the daughter of Leto.
She held the Greeks in check until,
as payment for the animal,
my father should offer his own daughter.
Hence, the sacrifice. There was no other
way.

He had to free the army,
to sail home or toward Troy.
These were the pressures that closed upon
    him.   [770]

He resisted, he hated it—
and then he killed her.
Not for Menelaos' sake, no, not at all.
But even if—let's say we grant your claim—
he did these things to help his brother,
was it right he should die for it at your
    hands?
By what law?
Watch out: this particular law
could recoil upon your own head.
If we made it a rule   [780]
to answer killing with killing,
you would die first,
in all justice.
Open your eyes! The claim is a fake.
Tell me:
Why do you live this way?
Your life is filth.
You share your bed with a bloodstained
    man:
once he obliged you by killing my father,
now you put him to use making children.   [790]
Once you had *decent* children from a *decent*
    father,
now you've thrown them out.
Am I supposed to praise that?
Or will you say

you do all this to avenge your child?
The thought is obscene—
to bed your enemies
and use a daughter as an alibi!
Oh why go on? I can't argue with you.
You have your one same answer ready: [800]
"That's no way to talk to your mother!"

Strange.
I don't think of you as mother at all.
You are some sort of punishment cage
locked around my life.
Evils from you, evils from him
are the air I breathe.
And what of Orestes?—he barely escaped
    you.
Poor boy.
The minutes are grinding him away
    somewhere.   [810]
You always accuse me
of training him up to be an avenger—
Oh I would if I could, you're so right!
Proclaim it to all!
Call me
baseminded, blackmouthing bitch! if you
    like—
for if this is my nature
we know how I come by it, don't we?

CHORUS   *[Looking at* KLYTAIMESTRA.*]*
Look. Anger is breathing out of her.

Yet she seems not to care   [820]
about right and wrong.

KLYTAIMESTRA   Right and wrong!
What use is that in dealing with her?
Do you hear her insults?
And this girl is old enough to know better.
The fact is, she would do *anything*,
don't you see that?
No shame at all.

ELEKTRA   Ah now there you mistake me.
Shame I do feel.   [830]
And I know there is something all wrong
        about me—
believe me. Sometimes I shock myself.
But there is a reason: you.
You never let up
this one same pressure of hatred on my
        life:
I am the shape you made me.
Filth teaches filth.

KLYTAIMESTRA   You little animal.
I and my deeds and my words draw
far too much comment from you.   [840]

ELEKTRA   You said it, not I.
For the deeds are your own.
But deeds find words for themselves,
don't they?

KLYTAIMESTRA   By Artemis I swear, you will pay for this
                when Aigisthos comes home!

ELEKTRA   See? You're out of control.
                Though you gave me permission to say
                        what I want,
                you don't know how to listen.

KLYTAIMESTRA   Silence! If you allow me   [850]
                I will proceed with my sacrifice.
                You spoke your piece.

ELEKTRA   Please! By all means! Go to it.
                Not another word from me.

KLYTAIMESTRA   *[To her attendant.]* You there! Yes you—lift up
                these offerings for me.
                I will offer prayers to this our king
                and loosen the fears that hold me now.
                Do you hear me, Apollo?
                I call you my champion!   [860]
                But my words are guarded, for I am not
                        among friends.
                It wouldn't do to unfold the whole tale
                with her standing here.
                She has a destroying tongue in her
                and she does love
                to sow wild stories all over town.
                So listen, I'll put it this way:
                last night was a night of bad dreams
                and ambiguous visions.

If they bode well for me, Lykian king, bring
    them to pass.   [870]
Otherwise, roll them back on my enemies!
And if there are certain people around
plotting to pull me down
from the wealth I enjoy,
do not allow it.
I want everything to go on as it is,
untroubled.
It suits me—this grand palace life
in the midst of my loved ones
and children—at least the ones   [880]
who do not bring me hatred and pain.

These are my prayers, Apollo.
Hear them.
Apollo,
grant them.
Gracious to all of us as we petition you.
And for the rest, though I keep silent,
I credit you with knowing it fully.
You are a god.
It goes without saying,   [890]
the children of Zeus see all things.
Amen.

[Enter the OLD MAN.*]*

OLD MAN   Ladies, can you tell me for certain
if this is the house of Aigisthos the king?

CHORUS   Yes, stranger, it is.

OLD MAN   And am I correct that this is his wife?
               She has a certain royal look.

CHORUS   Yes. That's who she is.

OLD MAN   Greetings, Queen. I have come with glad
                   tidings
               for you and Aigisthos, from a friend of
                   yours.   [900]

KLYTAIMESTRA   That's welcome news. But tell me
               who sent you.

OLD MAN   Phanoteus the Phokian. On a mission of
               some importance.

KLYTAIMESTRA   What mission? Tell me.
               Insofar as I like Phanoteus,
               I am likely to like your news.

OLD MAN   Orestes is dead. That is the sum of it.

ELEKTRA   OI 'GO TALAINA.
               My death begins now.

KLYTAIMESTRA   What are you saying, what are you saying?   [910]
               Don't bother with her.

OLD MAN   Orestes—dead. I say it again.

ELEKTRA   I am at the end. I exist no more.

KLYTAIMESTRA   *[To* ELEKTRA.*]* Mind your own affairs, girl.
                 But you, stranger—tell me the true story:
                 How did he die?

OLD MAN   Yes I was sent for this purpose, I'll tell the
                       whole thing.
                 Well:
                 he had gone to the spectacle at Delphi,
                 where all Greece turns up for the games.   [920]
                 Things were just beginning to get under
                       way
                 and the herald's voice rang out
                 announcing the footrace—first contest.
                 When he came onto the track
                 he was radiant. Every eye turned.
                 Well, he leveled the competition,
                 took first prize and came away famous.
                 Oh there's so much to tell—
                 I never saw anything like his
                       performance!—but
                 let me come straight to the point.   [930]
                 He won every contest the judges
                       announced—
                 single lap, double lap, pentathlon, you
                       name it.

                 First prize every time.
                 He was beginning to take on an aura.
                 His name rang out over the track again and
                       again:
                 "Argive Orestes,

whose father commanded the armies of
    Greece!"
So far so good.
But when a god sends harm,
no man can sidestep it,   [940]
no matter how strong he may be.
Came another day.
Sunrise: the chariot race.
He entered the lists.
What a pack:
there was one from Achaia,
a Spartan,
two Libyan drivers,
and he in the midst on Thessalian horses
stood fifth.   [950]
Sixth an Aitolian man, driving bays.
Seventh someone from Magnesia.
An Ainian man, riding white horses, had
    eighth place
and ninth a driver from godbuilt Athens.
Then a Boiotian.
Ten cars in all.
As they took their positions,
the judges cast lots to line up the cars.
A trumpet blast sounded.
They shot down the track.   [960]
All shouting together, reins tossing—

a hard clatter filled the whole course
and a vast float of dust
as they all streamed together,
each one lashing and straining ahead

to the next axle box, the next snorting lip,
and the horse foam flying
back over shoulders and wheels as they
    pounded past.
Meanwhile Orestes
just grazing the post each time with his
    wheel,   [970]
was letting his right horse go wide,
reining back on the other.
The cars were all upright at this point—

then, all of a sudden
the Ainian's colts go out of control
and swerve off
just as they round the seventh turn.
They crash head-on into the Barkaian team.
Then one car after another comes ramming
    into the pile
and the whole plain of Krisa   [980]
fills with the smoke of wrecks.
Now
the Athenian driver was smart, he saw

what was happening.
Drew offside and waited as
the tide of cars went thundering by.
Orestes
was driving in last place,
lying back on his mares.
He had put his faith in the finish.   [990]
But as soon as he sees
the Athenian driver alone on the track

he lets out a cry that shivers his horses' ears
and goes after him.
Neck and neck
they are racing,
first one, then
the other
nosing ahead,
easing ahead.   [1000]

Now our unlucky boy had stood every
        course so far,
sailing right on in his upright car,
but at this point he lets the left rein go slack
with the horses turning,
he doesn't notice,
hits the pillar and
smashes the axle box in two.
Out he flips
over the chariot rail,
reins snarled around him   [1010]
and as he falls
the horses scatter midcourse.
They see him down. A gasp goes through
        the crowd:
"Not the boy!"
To go for glory and end like this—
pounded against the ground,
legs beating the sky—
the other drivers could hardly manage
to stop his team and cut him loose.
Blood everywhere.   [1020]
He was unrecognizable. Sickening.

They burned him at once on a pyre
and certain Phokians are bringing
the mighty body back—
just ashes,
a little bronze urn—
so you can bury him in his father's ground.
That is my story.
So far as words go,
gruesome enough.   [1030]
But for those who watched it,
and we did watch it,
the ugliest evil I ever saw.

CHORUS   PHEU PHEU.
                The whole ancient race
                torn off at the roots. Gone.

KLYTAIMESTRA   Zeus! What now? Should I call this good
                    news?
                Or a nightmare cut to my own advantage?
                There is something grotesque
                in having my own evils save my life.   [1040]

OLD MAN   Why are you so disheartened at this news,
                    my lady?

KLYTAIMESTRA   To give birth is terrible, incomprehensible.
                No matter how you suffer,
                you cannot hate a child you've borne.

OLD MAN   My coming was futile then, it seems.

KLYTAIMESTRA   Futile? Oh no. How—
if you've come with convincing proof of his
      death?
He was alive because I gave him life.
But he chose to desert my breasts
      and my care,
to live as an exile, aloof and strange.   [1050]
After he left here he never saw me.
But he laid against me
the death of his father,
he made terrible threats.
And I had no shelter in sleep by night or
      sleep by day:
Time stood like a deathmaster over me,
letting the minutes drop.
Now I am free!
Today I shake loose from my fear
of her, my fear of him.   [1060]
And to tell you the truth,
she did more damage.
She lived in my house
and drank
my lifeblood neat!
Now things are different.
She may go on making threats—but
      so what?
From now on, I pass my days in peace.

ELEKTRA   OIMOI TALAINA.
Now I have grief enough to cry out
      OIMOI—   [1070]
Orestes! Poor cold thing.

As you lie in death
your own mother insults you.
What a fine sight!

KLYTAIMESTRA   Well you're no fine sight.
But he looks as fine as can be.

ELEKTRA   Nemesis! Hear her!

KLYTAIMESTRA   Nemesis *has* heard me. And she has
answered.

ELEKTRA   Batter away. This is your hour of luck.

KLYTAIMESTRA   And you think you will stop me,
you and Orestes?   [1080]

ELEKTRA   It is we who are stopped. There's no
stopping you.

KLYTAIMESTRA   Stranger, you deserve reward
if you really have put a stop on her traveling
tongue.

OLD MAN   Then I'll be on my way, if all is well.

KLYTAIMESTRA   Certainly not! You've earned better
of me and the man who dispatched you.
No, you go inside.
Just leave her out here
to go on with her evil litany.

[*Exit* KLYTAIMESTRA *and the* OLD MAN *into house.*]

ELEKTRA   Well how did she look to you—shattered by [1090]
               grief?
           Heartbroken mother bewailing her only son?
           No—you saw her—she went off laughing!
           O TALAIN'EGO.
           Orestes beloved,
           as you die you destroy me.
           You have torn away the part of my mind
           where hope was—
           my one hope in you
           to live,
           to come back,   [1100]
           to avenge us.
           Now where can I go?
           Alone I am.
           Bereft of you. Bereft of father.
           Should I go back into slavery?
           Back to those creatures who cut down my
               father?
           What a fine picture.
           No.
           I will not go back inside that house.
           No. At this door   [1110]
           I will let myself lie
           unloved.
           I will wither my life.
           If it aggravates them,
           they can kill me.
           Yes it will be a grace if I die.

To exist is pain.
Life is no desire of mine anymore.

CHORUS   Where are you lightnings of Zeus!
Where are you scorching Sun!   [1120]
In these dark pits you leave us dark!

ELEKTRA   E E AIAI.

CHORUS   Child, why do you cry?

ELEKTRA   PHEU.

CHORUS   Don't make that sound.

ELEKTRA   You will break me.

CHORUS   How?

ELEKTRA   If you bring me hope and I know he is dead,
you will harm my heart.

CHORUS   But think of Amphiaraus: [1130]
he was a king once,
snared by a woman in nets of gold.
Now under the earth

ELEKTRA   E E IO.

CHORUS   he is a king in the shadows of souls.

ELEKTRA   PHEU.

CHORUS   Cry PHEU, yes! For his murderess—

ELEKTRA   was destroyed!

CHORUS   Destroyed.

ELEKTRA   I know—because an avenger arose.   [1140]
           I have no such person. That person is gone.

CHORUS   You are a woman marked for sorrow.

ELEKTRA   Yes I know sorrow. Know it far too well.
           My life is a tunnel
           choked
           by the sweepings of dread.

CHORUS   We have watched you grieving.

ELEKTRA   Then do not try—

CHORUS   What?

ELEKTRA   To console me.   [1150]
           The fact is,
           there are no more hopes.
           No fine brothers.
           No comfort.

CHORUS   Death exists inside every mortal.

ELEKTRA   Oh yes, but think of the hooves drumming
                  down on him!

See that thing
dragging behind in the reins—

CHORUS   Too cruel.

ELEKTRA   Yes. Death made him a stranger—   [1160]

CHORUS   PAPAI.

ELEKTRA   Laid out
somewhere
not by my hands.
Not with my tears.

[Enter CHRYSOTHEMIS.]

CHRYSOTHEMIS   I am so happy, I ran here to tell you—
putting good manners aside!
I have good news for you that spells
release
from all your grieving.

ELEKTRA   Where could you find anything to touch
my grief?   [1170]
It has no cure.

CHRYSOTHEMIS   Orestes is with us—yes! Know it from me—
plain as you see me standing here!

ELEKTRA   You are mad.
You are joking.

CHRYSOTHEMIS   By the hearth of our father, this is no joke.
                He is with us. He is.

ELEKTRA   You poor girl.
                Who gave you this story?   [1180]

CHRYSOTHEMIS   No one gave me the story!
                I saw the evidence with my own eyes.

ELEKTRA   What evidence?
                My poor girl, what has set you on fire?

CHRYSOTHEMIS   Well listen, for gods' sake.
                Find out if I'm crazy or not.

ELEKTRA   All right, tell the tale, if it makes you happy.

CHRYSOTHEMIS   Yes, I will tell all I saw.
                Well.
                When I arrived at Father's grave
                I saw milk dripping down from the top of
                    the mound   [1190]
                and the tomb wreathed in flowers—
                flowers of every kind—what a shock!
                I peered all around—
                in case someone was sneaking up on me
                but no, the whole place was perfectly still.
                I crept near the tomb.
                And there it was.
                Right there on the edge.
                A lock of hair, fresh cut.
                As soon as I saw it, a bolt went through me— [1200]

almost as if I saw his face,
I suddenly knew! Orestes.
Beloved Orestes.
I lifted it up. I said not a word.
I was weeping for joy.
And I know it now as I knew it then,
this offering had to come from him.
Who else would bother, except you
   or me?
And I didn't do it. I'm sure of that.
You couldn't do it—god knows you don't   [1210]
take a step from this house without getting
   in trouble.
And certainly Mother has no such
   inclinations.

If she did, we would hear of it.
No, I tell you these offerings came from
   Orestes.
Oh Elektra, lift your heart!
Bad luck can't last forever.
Long have we lived in shadows and
   shuddering:
today I think our future is opening out.

ELEKTRA   PHEU!
Poor lunatic. I feel sorry for you.   [1220]

CHRYSOTHEMIS   What do you mean? Why aren't you happy?

ELEKTRA   You're dreaming, girl, lost in a moving
   dream.

CHRYSOTHEMIS   Dreaming! How? I saw what I saw!

ELEKTRA   He is dead, my dear one.
He's not going to save you.
Dead, do you hear me? Dead. Forget him.

CHRYSOTHEMIS   OIMOI TALAINA.
Who told you that?

ELEKTRA   Someone who was there when he died.

CHRYSOTHEMIS   And where is this someone? It's all so
strange.   [1230]

ELEKTRA   He's gone in the house. To entertain
Mother.

CHRYSOTHEMIS   I don't want to hear this. I don't understand.
Who put those offerings on Father's tomb?

ELEKTRA   I think, most likely, someone who wished
to honor Orestes' memory.

CHRYSOTHEMIS   What a fool I am—here I come racing for
joy
to tell you my news, with no idea
how things really are.
The evils multiply.

ELEKTRA   Yes they do. But listen to me.   [1240]
You could ease our sorrow.

CHRYSOTHEMIS   How? Raise the dead?

ELEKTRA   That's not what I meant. I am not quite
insane.

CHRYSOTHEMIS   Then what do you want? Am I capable of it?

ELEKTRA   All you need is the nerve—to do what I say.

CHRYSOTHEMIS   If it benefits us, I will not refuse.

ELEKTRA   But you know nothing succeeds without
work.

CHRYSOTHEMIS   I do. I'll give you all the strength I have.

ELEKTRA   Good then, listen. Here is my plan.
You know, I think, our present contingent
of allies: zero.   [1250]
Death took them.
We two are alone.
Up to now, while I heard that my brother
was living
I cherished a hope
that he'd arrive one day to avenge his father.
But Orestes
no longer exists. I look to you.
You will not shrink back.
You will stand with your sister
and put to death the man who murdered
your father: [1260]
Aigisthos.

After all, what are you waiting for?
Let's be blunt, girl, what hope is left?
Your losses are mounting,
the property gone and
marriage
seems a fading dream at your age—
or do you still console yourself with
        thoughts of a husband?
Forget it. Aigisthos is not so naive   [1270]
as to see children born from you or from
        me—
unambiguous grief for himself.
But now if you join in my plans,
you will win, in the first place,
profound and sacred respect from the dead
        below:
your father, your brother.
And second, people will call you noble.
That is your lineage, that is your future.
And besides, you will find a husband,
a good one: men like a woman with
        character.   [1280]
Oh don't you see? You'll make us famous!
People will cheer! They'll say
"Look at those two!" They'll say
"Look at the way they saved their father's
        house!
Against an enemy standing strong!
Risked their lives! Stood up to murder!
Those two deserve to be honored in public,
on every streetcorner and festival in the
        city—

there should be a prize for heroism like
    that!"
So they will speak of us.   [1290]
And whether we live or die doesn't matter:
that fame will stand.
Oh my dear one, listen to me.
Take on your father's work,
take up your brother's task,
make some refuge from evil for me
and for you.
Because you know,
there is a kind of excellence
in me and you—born in us—   [1300]
and it cannot live in shame.

CHORUS   In times like these, speaking or listening,
          forethought is your ally.

CHRYSOTHEMIS   Well yes—and if this were a rational woman
               she would have stopped to think before she
                   spoke.
               She is, unfortunately, mad.
               Tell me, what in the world do you have in
                   mind
               as you throw on your armor
               and call me to your side?
               Look at yourself! You are female,   [1310]
               not male—born that way.
               And you're no match for them in strength
                   or in luck.
               They are flush with fortune;
               our luck has trickled away.

Really, Elektra,
who would think to topple a man of his
    stature?
Who could ever get away with it?
Be careful: this sort of blundering
might make things worse for us—
what if someone overhears!   [1320]
And there is nothing whatever to win or to
    gain
if we make ourselves famous and die in
    disgrace.
Death itself is not the worst thing.
Worse is to live
when you want to die.
So I beg you,
before you destroy us
and wipe out the family altogether,
control your temper.
As for your words,   [1330]
I will keep them secret—for your sake.
Oh Elektra, get some sense! It is almost
    too late.
Your strength is nothing. You cannot beat
    them: give up.

CHORUS   Hear that? Foresight!—
no greater asset a person can have
than foresight combined with good sense.

ELEKTRA   Predictable.
I knew you'd say no.
Well: [1340]

alone then.
One hand will have to be enough.
One hand *is* enough.
Yes.

CHRYSOTHEMIS   Too bad you weren't so resolved
on the day Father died.
You could have finished the task.

ELEKTRA   Yes, I had the guts for it then, but no
strategy.

CHRYSOTHEMIS   Forget strategy—you'll live longer.

ELEKTRA   I gather you don't intend to help.   [1350]

CHRYSOTHEMIS   Too risky for me.

ELEKTRA   You have your own strategy, I see.
I admire that.
But your cowardice appalls me.

CHRYSOTHEMIS   One day you will say I was right.

ELEKTRA   Never.

CHRYSOTHEMIS   The future will judge.

ELEKTRA   Oh go away. You give no help.

CHRYSOTHEMIS   You take no advice.

ELEKTRA   Why not run off and tell all this to Mother?   [1360]

CHRYSOTHEMIS   I don't hate you that much.

ELEKTRA   At least realize you are driving me into
             dishonor.

CHRYSOTHEMIS   Dishonor? No: foresight.

ELEKTRA   And I should conform to your version of
             justice?

CHRYSOTHEMIS   When you are sane, you can think for us
                  both.

ELEKTRA   Terrible to sound so right and be so
             wrong.

CHRYSOTHEMIS   Well put! You describe yourself to a fault.

ELEKTRA   Do you deny that I speak for justice?

CHRYSOTHEMIS   Let's just say there are times
                  when justice is too big a risk.   [1370]

ELEKTRA   I will not live by rules like those.

CHRYSOTHEMIS   Go ahead then. You'll find out I was right.

ELEKTRA   I *do* go ahead. You cannot deter me.

CHRYSOTHEMIS   So you won't change your plan?

ELEKTRA   Immorality isn't a plan. It is the enemy.

CHRYSOTHEMIS   You don't hear a single word I say.

ELEKTRA   Oh it was all decided long ago.

CHRYSOTHEMIS   Well I'll be off.
                It's clear you could never bring yourself
                to praise my words, nor I your ways.   [1380]

ELEKTRA   Yes. You do that. You be off.
                But I will not follow you,
                no.
                Never.
                Not even if you beg me.
                When
                I look in your eyes I see emptiness.

CHRYSOTHEMIS   If that is your attitude,
                that is your attitude.
                When you're in deep trouble,   [1390]
                you'll say I was right.

                [Exit CHRYSOTHEMIS.]

CHORUS   Why is it—
                we look at birds in the air,
                we see it makes sense
                the way they care
                for the life of those who sow and sustain
                    them—
                why

is it
we don't do the same?
No: [1400]
by lightning of Zeus,
by Themis of heaven,
not long

free of pain!
O
sound going down
to the dead in the
ground,
take a voice,
take my voice,   [1410]
take down
pity
below
to Atreus' dead:
tell them shame.
Tell them there is no dancing.

Because
here is a house falling sick
falling now
between two children battling,   [1420]
and there is no more level of love in the
    days.
Betrayed,
alone
she goes down in the waves:
Elektra,
grieving for death,

for her father,
as a nightingale
grieving always.
Nor   [1430]
does she think
to fear dying,
no!
she is glad
to go dark.
As a
killer
of Furies,
as a pureblooded
child   [1440]
of the father who sowed her.
No one wellborn
is willing to live

with evil,
with shame,
with a name made nameless.
O child,
child,
you made your life a wall of tears
against dishonor: [1450]
you fought and you won.
For they call you
the child of his mind,

child of his excellence.
I pray you raise your hand
and crush the ones

who now
crush you!
For I see you subsisting
in mean part,   [1460]
and yet
you are one who kept faith
with the living laws,
kept faith
in the clear reverence
of Zeus.

[Enter ORESTES *and* PYLADES *with urn.]*

ORESTES   Tell me ladies, did we get the right
                    directions?
           Are we on the right road? Is this the place?

CHORUS   What place? What do you want?

ORESTES   The place where Aigisthos lives.   [1470]

CHORUS   Well here you are. Your directions were
                    good.

ORESTES   Which one of you, then, will tell those
                    within?
           Our arrival will please them.

CHORUS   Her—as nearest of kin, she is the right one
           to announce you.

ORESTES   Please, my lady, go in and tell them
           that certain Phokians are asking for
                Aigisthos.

ELEKTRA   OIMOI TALAIN'.
           Oh no. Don't say that. Don't say you have
                come with
           evidence of the stories we heard.   [1480]

ORESTES   I don't know what you heard.
           Old Strophios sent me with news of
                Orestes.

ELEKTRA   Oh stranger, what news? Fear comes
                walking into me.

ORESTES   We have his remains in a small urn here—
           for he's dead, as you see.

ELEKTRA   OI 'GO TALAINA.
           Oh no. No. Not this thing in your hands.
           No.

ORESTES   If you have tears to shed for Orestes,
           this urn is all that holds his body now.   [1490]

ELEKTRA   Oh stranger, allow me, in gods' name—
           if this vessel does really contain him,
           to hold it in my hands.
           For myself, for the whole generation of us,
           I have tears to keep,
           I have ashes to weep.

ORESTES *[To* PYLADES *with urn.]* Bring it here, give it
                 to her, whoever she is.
                 It is no enemy asking this.
                 She is someone who loved him,
                 or one of his blood.   [1500]

ELEKTRA If this were all you were, Orestes,
                 how could your memory
                 fill my memory,
                 how is it your soul fills my soul?
                 I sent you out, I get you back:
                 tell me
                 how could the difference be simply
                 nothing?
                 Look!
                 You are nothing at all.   [1510]
                 Just a crack where the light slipped
                       through.
                 Oh my child,
                 I thought I could save you.
                 I thought I could send you beyond.
                 But there is no beyond.
                 You might as well have stayed that day
                 to share your father's tomb.
                 Instead, somewhere, I don't know where—
                 suddenly alone you stopped—
                 where death was.   [1520]
                 You stopped.
                 And I would have waited
                 and washed you
                 and lifted you
                 up from the fire,

like a whitened coal.
Strangers are so careless!
Look how you got smaller, coming back.
OIMOI TALAINA.
All my love   [1530]
gone for nothing.
Days of my love, years of my love.
Into your child's fingers I put the earth and
    the sky.
No mother did that for you.
No nurse.
No slave.
I. Your sister
without letting go,
day after day, year after year,
and you my own sweet child.   [1540]

But death was a wind too strong for that.

One day three people vanished.
Father. You. Me. Gone.
Now our enemies rock with laughter.
And she runs mad for joy—
that creature
in the shape of your mother—
how often you said you would come
one secret evening and cut her throat!
But our luck canceled that,   [1550]
whatever luck is.
And instead my beloved,
luck sent you back to me
colder than ashes,

later than shadow.
OIMOI MOI.
Pity,
PHEU PHEU
oh beloved,
OIMOI MOI   [1560]
as you vanish down that road.
Oh my love
take me there.
Let me dwell where you are.
I am already nothing.
I am already burning.
Oh my love, I was once part of you—
take me too!
Only void is between us.
And I see that the dead feel no pain.   [1570]

CHORUS   Elektra, be reasonable.
          Your father was a mortal human being.
          Orestes too—we all pay the same price for
               that.
          Control yourself.

ORESTES   PHEU PHEU.
          What should I say? This is
          impossible! I cannot hold my tongue much
               longer.

ELEKTRA   What is the matter? What are you trying to
               say?

ORESTES   Is this the brilliant Elektra?

ELEKTRA　This is Elektra. Brilliant no more.　　　[1580]

ORESTES　OIMOI TALAINES.
　　　　　It hurts me to look at you.

ELEKTRA　Surely, stranger, you're not feeling sorry for
　　　　　me?

ORESTES　It shocks me, the way you look: Do they
　　　　　abuse you?

ELEKTRA　Yes, in fact. But who are you?

ORESTES　PHEU.
　　　　　What an ugly, loveless life for a girl.

ELEKTRA　Why do you stare at me? Why are you so
　　　　　sympathetic?

ORESTES　I had no idea how bad my situation
　　　　　really is.

ELEKTRA　And what makes you realize that?
　　　　　Something I said?　　　[1590]

ORESTES　Just to see the outline of your suffering.

ELEKTRA　Yet this is only a fraction of it you see.

ORESTES　What could be worse than this?

ELEKTRA　To live in the same house with killers.

ORESTES   What killers? What evil are you hinting at?

ELEKTRA   My own father's killers.
               And I serve them as a slave. By compulsion.

ORESTES   Who compels you?

ELEKTRA   Mother she is called. Mother she is not.

ORESTES   How do you mean? Does she strike you?
               Insult you?   [1600]

ELEKTRA   Yes. And worse.

ORESTES   But have you no one to protect you?
               No one to stand in her way?

ELEKTRA   No. There was someone. Here are his
                   ashes.

ORESTES   Oh girl. How I pity the dark life you live.

ELEKTRA   No one else has ever pitied me, you know.

ORESTES   No one else has ever been part of your
                   grief.

ELEKTRA   Do you mean you are somehow part of my
                   family?

ORESTES   I'll explain—if these women are
                   trustworthy.

ELEKTRA   Oh yes, you can trust them. Speak freely.   [1610]

ORESTES   Give back the urn, then, and you will hear
          everything.

ELEKTRA   No! Don't take this from me, for gods' sake,
          whoever you are!

ORESTES   Come now, do as I say. It is the right thing.

ELEKTRA   No! In all reverence no please—don't take
              this away.
          It is all that I love.

ORESTES   I forbid you to keep it.

ELEKTRA   O TALAIN'EGO SETHEN.
          Orestes! What if
          they take from me   [1620]
          even the rites of your death!

ORESTES   Hush, now. That language is wrong.

ELEKTRA   Wrong to mourn my own dead brother?

ORESTES   Wrong for you to say that word.

ELEKTRA   How did I lose the right to call him
              brother?

ORESTES   Your rights you have. Your brother you
              don't.

ELEKTRA   Do I not stand here with Orestes himself in
            my hands?

ORESTES   No, in fact. That Orestes is a lie.

ELEKTRA   Then where in the world is the poor boy's
            grave?

ORESTES   Nowhere. The living need no grave.   [1630]

ELEKTRA   Child, what are you saying?

ORESTES   Nothing but the truth.

ELEKTRA   The man is alive?

ORESTES   As I live and breathe.

ELEKTRA   You—?

ORESTES   Look at this ring—our father's—

ELEKTRA   Father's!

ORESTES   —and see what I mean.

ELEKTRA   Oh love, you break on me like light!

ORESTES   Yes like light!   [1640]

ELEKTRA   Oh voice, have you come out of nowhere?

ORESTES   Nowhere but where you are.

ELEKTRA   Do I hold you now in my hands?

ORESTES   Now and forever.

ELEKTRA   Ladies, my friends, my people, look!
           Here stands Orestes:
           dead by device
           now by device brought back to life!

CHORUS   I see, child. And at this reversal,
           my tears are falling for joy.   [1650]

ELEKTRA   IO GONAI.
           You exist!
           You came back,
           you found me—

ORESTES   Yes, I am here. Now keep silent awhile.

ELEKTRA   Why?

ORESTES   Silence is better. Someone inside might
               overhear.

ELEKTRA   By Artemis unbroken! I would not
           dignify with fear
           the dull surplus of females   [1660]
           who huddle in that house!

ORESTES   Careful! There is war in women too,
            as you know by experience, I think.

ELEKTRA   OTOTOTOTOI TOTOI.
            You drive me back down my desperation—
            that unclouded
            incurable
            never forgotten
            evil
            growing inside my life.   [1670]

ORESTES   I know, but we should talk of those deeds
            when the moment is right.

ELEKTRA   Every arriving moment of my life
            has a right
            to tell those deeds!
            And this chance to speak freely is hard-won.

ORESTES   Precisely. Safeguard it.

ELEKTRA   How?

ORESTES   When the time is unsuitable, no long
                  speeches.

ELEKTRA   But how could silence be the right way to
                  greet   [1680]
            you—simply
            coming
            out of nowhere
            like a miracle?

ORESTES It was a miracle set in motion by the gods.

ELEKTRA Ah.
That is a vast claim
and much more beautiful,
to think
some god   [1690]
has brought you here.
Some god: yes! That must be true.

ORESTES Elektra, I do not like to curb your rejoicing
but I am afraid when you lose control.

ELEKTRA Oh but my love—
now that you have traveled back down all
    those years
to meet my heart,
over all this grief of mine,
do not
oh love—   [1700]

ORESTES What are you asking?

ELEKTRA Do not turn your face from me.
Don't take yourself away.

ORESTES Of course not. No one else will take me
    either.

ELEKTRA Do you mean that?

ORESTES Yes I do.

ELEKTRA   Oh beloved,
           I heard your voice
           when I had no hope
           and my heart leapt away from me   [1710]
           calling
           you.
           I was in sorrow.
           But now
           I am holding you,
           now you are visible—
           light of the face I could never forget.

ORESTES   Spare me these words.
           You don't need to teach me my mother is
               evil
           or how Aigisthos drains the family wealth,   [1720]
           pours it out like water,
           sows it to the wind.
           We've no time for all that—talk is
               expensive.
           What I need now are the practical details:
           where we should hide, where we can leap
               out
           and push that enemy laughter
           right back down their throats!
           But be careful she doesn't read
           the fact of our presence
           straight from the glow on your face.   [1730]
           You must keep on lamenting
           my fictitious death.
           Time enough

for lyres and laughter   ]
when we've won the day.

ELEKTRA   Your will and my will are one: identical,
              brother.
          For I take all my joy from you,
          none is my own.
          Nor could I harm you ever so slightly
          at any price: it would be a disservice   [1740]
          to the god who stands beside us now.
          So. You know what comes next.
          Aigisthos has gone out,
          Mother is home.
          And don't worry:
          she'll see no glow on my face.
          Hatred put out the light in me a long time
              ago.
          Besides, since I saw you
          my tears keep running down—
          tears, joy, tears all mixed up together.   [1750]
          How could I stop?
          I saw you come down that road a dead man,
          I looked again and saw you alive.
          You have used me strangely.
          Why—if Father suddenly came back
              to life
          I wouldn't call it fantastic.
          Believe what you see.
          But
          now you have come,
          I am yours to command.   [1760]

Alone,
I would have done one of two things:
deliver myself or else die.

ORESTES   Quiet! I hear someone coming out.

ELEKTRA   Go inside, strangers.
You are bringing a gift
they can neither reject nor rejoice in.

[Enter the OLD MAN.*]*

OLD MAN   Idiots! Have you lost your wits completely,
and your instinct to survive as well—
or were you born brainless?   [1770]
You're not on the brink of disaster now,
you're right in the eye of it, don't you see
        that?
Why, except for me standing guard at the
        door here
this long while, your plans
would have been in the house
before yourselves!
Good thing I took caution.
Now cut short the speechmaking,
stifle your joy
and go into the house. Go!   [1780]
Delay is disaster in things like this.
Get it over with: that's the point now.

ORESTES   How will I find things inside?

OLD MAN Perfect. No one will know you.

ORESTES You reported me dead?

OLD MAN You are deep in hell, so far as they know.

ORESTES Are they happy at this?

OLD MAN I'll tell you that later. For now,
the whole plan is unfolding beautifully.
Even the ugly parts.   [1790]

ELEKTRA Who is this man, brother?

ORESTES Don't you know him?

ELEKTRA Not even remotely.

ORESTES You don't know the man into whose hands
you put me,
once long ago?

ELEKTRA What man? What are you saying?

ORESTES The man who smuggled me off to Phokis,
thanks to your foresight.

ELEKTRA Him? Can it be? That man was
the one trustworthy soul I could find in the
house,   [1800]
the day Father died!

ORESTES   That's who he is. Do not question me
          further.

ELEKTRA   *[To the* OLD MAN.*]* I bless you like the light
          of day!
    I bless you
    as the savior of the house of Agamemnon!
    How did you come? Is it really you—
    who pulled us up from the pit that day?
    I bless your hands,
    I bless your feet,
    I bless the sweet roads you walked!   [1810]
    How strange
    you were beside me all that time and gave
        no sign.
    Strange—to destroy me with lies
    when you had such sweet truth to tell.
    Bless you, Father!—Yes, Father.
    That is who I see when I look at you now.

    There is no man on earth I have hated and
        loved like you
    on the one same day.

OLD MAN   Enough, now. As for all the stories in
          between—
    there will be nights and days   [1820]
    to unravel them, Elektra.
    But for you two, standing here,
    I have just one word: act!
    Now is the moment!
    Now Klytaimestra is alone.

Now there is not one man in the house.
If you wait you will have to fight others,
more skilled and more numerous. Think!

ORESTES   Well, Pylades, no more speeches.
           As quick as we can   [1830]
           into the house—after
           we pay our respects
           to the gods of this doorway.

           [*Exit* ORESTES *and* PYLADES *followed by the*
           OLD MAN.]

ELEKTRA   King Apollo! Graciously hear them.
           Hear me too! I have been devout,
           I have come to you often,
           bringing you gifts of whatever I had.
           Now again I come with all that I have:
           Apollo wolfkiller! I beg you!
           I call out—   [1840]
           I fall to my knees!
           please send your mind over us,
           inform our strategies,
           show
           how the gods reward
           unholy action!

CHORUS   Look where he comes grazing forward,
           blood bubbling over his lips: Ares!
           As a horizontal scream into the house
           go the hunters of evil,   [1850]
           the raw and deadly dogs.

Not long now:
the blazing dream of my head is crawling
    out.

Here he comes like a stealing shadow,
like a footprint of death into the rooms,
stalking the past

with freshcut blood in his hands.
It is Hermes who guides him
down a blindfold of shadow—
straight to the finish line: not long now!   [1860]

ELEKTRA   My ladies! The men
are about to accomplish the deed—
be silent and wait.

CHORUS   How? What are they doing?

ELEKTRA   She is dressing the urn. They are standing
    beside her.

CHORUS   But why did you come running out here?

ELEKTRA   To watch that Aigisthos doesn't surprise us.

KLYTAIMESTRA   [within] AIAI IO.
Rooms
filled with murder!   [1870]

ELEKTRA   Someone inside screams—do you hear?

CHORUS   Yes I hear. It makes my skin crawl.

KLYTAIMESTRA OIMOI TALAIN'.
              Aigisthos, where are you?

ELEKTRA   There! Again! Someone calls out.

KLYTAIMESTRA Oh child my child, pity the mother who
                  bore you!

ELEKTRA   Yet you had little enough pity for him
              and none for his father!

CHORUS   Alas for the city.
              Alas for a whole race thrown and shattered: [1880]
              the shape that followed you down the days
              is dying now, dying away.

KLYTAIMESTRA OMOI.
              I am hit!

ELEKTRA   Hit her a second time, if you have the
                  strength!

KLYTAIMESTRA OMOI MAL' AUTHIS.
              Again!

ELEKTRA   If only Aigisthos could share this!

CHORUS   The curses are working.
              Under the ground   [1890]

dead men are alive
with their black lips moving,
black mouths sucking
on the soles of killers' feet.

Here they come,
hands soaked with red: Ares is happy!
Enough said.

ELEKTRA   Orestes, how does it go?

ORESTES   Good, so far—at least so far as Apollo's
           oracle was good.

ELEKTRA   Is the creature dead?   [1900]

ORESTES   Your good mother will not insult you
           anymore.

CHORUS   Stop! I see Aigisthos coming, yes, it is him.

ELEKTRA   Boys, get back!

ORESTES   Where do you see him—

ELEKTRA   There—marching right down on us
           full of joy.

CHORUS   Go quick to the place just inside the front
              door.
           You have won the first round. Now for the
              second.

ORESTES   Don't worry. We will finish this.

ELEKTRA   Hurry. Go to it.   [1910]

ORESTES   Yes I am gone.

ELEKTRA   And leave this part to me.

CHORUS   Why not drop a few friendly words in his
                  ear—
            so his moment of justice may come
            as a surprise.

            [Enter AIGISTHOS.*]*

AIGISTHOS   Does anyone know where those Phokian
                  strangers are?
            People say they have news of Orestes
            dead in a chariot crash.
            You!
            yes you!—you've never been shy   [1920]
            to speak your mind.
            And obviously this matter most concerns
                  you.

ELEKTRA   Yes of course I know, for I do keep track
            of the fortunes of the family.

AIGISTHOS   Where are they then,
            the strangers?—tell me.

ELEKTRA   Inside the house, for they've fallen upon
                the perfect hostess.

AIGISTHOS   And it's true they bring a report of his
                    death?

ELEKTRA   No—better: they have evidence,   [1930]
                not just words.

AIGISTHOS   We can see proof?

ELEKTRA   You can, indeed, though it's no pretty sight.

AIGISTHOS   Well this is good news. Unusual, coming
                    from you.

ELEKTRA   Relish it while you can.

AIGISTHOS   Silence! I say throw open the gates!
                for every Mykenaian and Argive to see—
                in case you had placed empty hopes
                in this man—
                take my bit on your tongue   [1940]
                or learn the hard way.

ELEKTRA   As for me, I am playing my part to the
                    end.
                I've learned to side with the winners.

                [A shrouded corpse is disclosed with ORESTES *and*
                PYLADES *standing beside it.]*

AIGISTHOS   O Zeus! I see here a man fallen by the
    jealousy of god
  —but
  if that remark offends,
  I unsay it.

  Uncover the eyes. Uncover it all.
  I should pay my respects.

ORESTES   Uncover it yourself.   [1950]
  This isn't my corpse—it's yours.
  Yours to look at, yours to eulogize.

AIGISTHOS   Yes good point. I have to agree.
  You there—Klytaimestra must be about in
    the house—
  call her for me.

ORESTES   She is right here before you. No need to
    look elsewhere.

AIGISTHOS   OIMOI.
  What do I see!

ORESTES   You don't know the face?

AIGISTHOS   Caught! But *who set the trap?*   [1960]

ORESTES   Don't you realize yet
  that you're talking to dead men alive?

AIGISTHOS   OIMOI.
I do understand. You are Orestes.

ORESTES   At last.

AIGISTHOS   I'm a dead man. No way out.
But let me just say—

ELEKTRA   No!
Don't let him speak—
by the gods! Brother—no speechmaking
    now!   [1970]
When a human being is so steeped in evil as
    this one
what is gained by delaying his death?
Kill him at once.
Throw his corpse out
for scavengers to get.
Nothing less than this
can cut the knot of evils
inside me.

ORESTES   Get in with you, quickly.
This is no word game: [1980]
your life is at stake.

AIGISTHOS   Why take me inside?
If the deed is honorable, what need of
    darkness?
You aren't ready to kill?

ORESTES   Don't give me instructions, just get yourself
                 in:
            You will die on the spot
            where you slaughtered my father.

AIGISTHOS   Must these rooms see
            the whole evil of Pelops' race,
            present and future?   [1990]

ORESTES   They will see yours, I can prophesy.

AIGISTHOS   That is no skill you got from your father!

ORESTES   Your answers are quick, your progress slow.
            Go.

AIGISTHOS   You lead the way.

ORESTES   No you go first.

AIGISTHOS   Afraid I'll escape?

ORESTES   You shall not die on your own terms.
            I will make it bitter for you.
            And let such judgment fall   [2000]
            on any who wish to break the law:
            kill them!
            The sum of evil will be less.

            [*Exit* ORESTES *and* AIGISTHOS, *followed by*
            ELEKTRA, *into the house.*]

CHORUS   O seed of Atreus:
          you suffered and broke free,

          you took aim and struck;
          you have won your way through
          to the finish line.

          [Exit CHORUS.*]*

ORESTES

by Euripides

INTRODUCTION

The wounded cry as the clown
Doubles his meaning . . .

—W. H. AUDEN

When we first meet Orestes in *Orestes*, he is asleep onstage. This sets up a relationship between us and him that will continue through the play. To see Orestes flounder about in decisions and actions as the story proceeds is like watching someone twitch in his sleep and let out the occasional scream. He is present but opaque to us—driven by a dream of his own life that is nightmarishly clear to him on the inside but which he never communicates to us. We see flashes of his reasoning lit up by this or that crisis but we get no sense of the plan of his mind. His moral reactions are often bizarre, as when Tyndareus, grandfather of Orestes and father of Klytaimestra, denounces him for having murdered his mother. Orestes' response is:

As a matter of fact, isn't it all your fault for engendering her?
You ruined me!
(447–48)

All in all, Orestes is a peculiar customer—not exactly insane but strange and unknowable. His consciousness is entirely his own. And in this respect he is a typical Euripidean creation. Euripides introduced to the Greek tragic stage a concern for the solitary, inward self, for consciousness as a private content that might or might not match up with the outside appearance of a person, that might or might not make sense to an observer. He lived at a time when philosophers as well as artists were becoming intrigued by this difference between outside and inside, appearance and reality, and were advancing various theories about what truth is and where truth lies. As a tragic poet, Euripides had to confront a special version of the problem. Within a traditional poetic form like Greek tragedy, the truth has only one definition: it is identical with myth. The truth about Orestes was contained in the standard myth of his adventures. Euripides could rearrange its details but he was not at liberty to stage a play in which Orestes refrained from killing his mother. That would have been seen as absurd and untrue. Nor could Euripides present a play that did not have three speaking actors, a chorus of average citizens and a divine epiphany at the end. These were the parts of a legitimate tragedy. Yet we sense in all of Euripides' playwriting a mind out of patience with this straitjacket of fixed truths and predictable procedures. He has revolutionary instincts. He wants to shatter and shock. He goes about it subversively. Leaving the external structure of the myth and the traditional form of the play intact, he allows everything inside to go a tiny bit awry. It creates a mad tension between content and form that builds to a point of explosion in the final scene.

So, for example, he uses the chorus, as was conventional, to comment on the action but he has them say incoherent or contradictory things from one choral ode to the next. He employs the standard device of a messenger speech to convey offstage events yet he employs it not once but twice and the second messenger is a sort of hysterical Trojan version of Venus Xtravaganza—a eunuch slave who speaks entirely in lyric verse (in the original production he would have sung his lines, probably soprano, to the accompaniment of a flute). Euripides throws in the eunuch for shock value and to make the end of the play more exasperating. He seems to prefer maximum exasperation in the final scene, where all the lines of the plot have been pushed to impasse and categories like good/evil, happy/unhappy, mortal/immortal are sliding around so crazily that only a god can make things clear.

So he brings on a god to make things clear, the deus ex machina being a conventional way of tying off the ends of a Greek tragedy. But here too form and content are at odds. For the god in question (it is Apollo) dictates a series of solutions that make nonsense of all the actions and anguish of the characters up to that point. For example, he instructs Orestes, who happens to be holding his sword to the throat of a young girl named Hermione, to lower his weapon and marry her. Orestes merrily agrees to do so.

How should we read moments like this, where exasperation verges on farce? Sometimes I wonder if Euripides saw the very texture of reality as ironic. Saw the gods as ironic. Saw the gods in their interactions with human beings as essentially *playing*. A frightening idea. But at least it entails the assumption that Euripides himself was *not* playing. That he was a serious playwright who knew his target and took aim.

Another serious way to read a play like *Orestes* is as an indictment of the age and the society in which the playwright lived.

His was a time of constant warfare, imperialist greed and aston-
ishing political corruption, rather like our own. Euripides pro-
duced *Orestes* in 408 B.C. Later the same year, he left Athens
and went to Macedonia, where he died in less than two years.
There is no historical evidence to explain why a highly successful
playwright would go into voluntary exile at the age of seventy-
three. But it makes *Orestes* his last statement to the Athenians—
and a wild, heartless, unconstruable statement it is. If I take it as
a story of real people, I can find no character to *like* in the play.
On the other hand, as an allegory or abstract design, it lacks all
exactitude—seems to unfold like a bolt of cloth falling down
stairs, spilling itself, random. Yet again, isn't there something terrible in randomness—the idea that at the very bottom of its cal-
culations, real depravity has no master plan of any kind, it's just a
dreamy whim that slides out of people when they are trapped or
bored or too lazy to analyze their own mania.

There is another way to read Euripides, which is to forget se-
riousness and see him as just having a good time in the theater,
creating sensation and spectacle, throwing the pieces up in the air
and letting them fall. To judge from some sentences in *Poetics*,
this was Aristotle's view. Still, Aristotle insists that whatever the
ineptitudes of his stagecraft, Euripides is TRAGIKOTATOS,
"the most tragic" of the Greek poets. A clown, but a dark clown.
A child, but terrific. At the start of this introduction I quoted
two lines of W. H. Auden that (although he is talking about
Shakespeare) seem to capture exactly how it feels to read or
watch Euripides' *Orestes*. Here is the whole stanza:

> *The aged catch their breath,*
> *For the nonchalant couple go*
> *Waltzing across the tightrope*
> *As if there were no death*

Or hope of falling down;
The wounded cry as the clown
Doubles his meaning, and O
How the dear little children laugh
When the drums roll and the lovely
Lady is sawn in half.[1]

---

1. It is the first stanza of Auden's preface to *The Sea and the Mirror*. In W. H. Auden, *Collected Poems*, ed. Edward Mendelson (New York: Knopf, 1991), 401.

DRAMATIS PERSONAE

(in order of appearance)

ELEKTRA	*daughter of Klytaimestra and Agamemnon*
HELEN	*wife of Menelaos*
CHORUS	*of women of Argos*
ORESTES	*son of Klytaimestra and Agamemnon*
MENELAOS	*brother of Agamemnon, husband of Helen*
TYNDAREUS	*father of Klytaimestra and Helen*
PYLADES	*Orestes' friend, silent no more*
MESSENGER	
HERMIONE	*daughter of Helen*
TROJAN SLAVE	*eunuch of Helen's entourage*
APOLLO	*god of light and law*

SETTING: *The action is set in Argos. Orestes lies on a bed in front of the house of Atreus, where he has recently murdered his mother, Klytaimestra, to avenge her murder of his father, Agamemnon. Elektra sits beside him.*

ELEKTRA Whatever dooms there are men die,
whatever harms there are men have—
Godsent: they blast, we bend.
Take Tantalos. It's a known fact
he was born of Zeus—*lucky there* (pardon
     my sarcasm)—
now he lives crouched in fear.
They hung up a boulder over his head.
Payback. It's a known fact,
when the gods asked him to dinner he shot
     off his mouth.
So Tantalos begot Pelops, Pelops begot
     Atreus—   [10]
you know all this don't you? the strife, the
     crimes,
Atreus slicing Pelops' children into soup—
and Atreus (I'm skipping some details)
     begot
Agamemnon (a.k.a. the Glorious)
as well as Menelaos, who married
     loathsome Helen.
Then Agamemnon found himself a wife
     (Klytaimestra)
and here we are: their offspring—three girls
     one boy.

Orestes, Chrysothemis, Iphigeneia, Elektra
      (me).
As for our father, well, Klytaimestra
      disposed of him.
Trapped him in a rug and slit his throat.   [20]
Motive?
I'm an innocent girl. Let's leave her motives
      blank.
But it seemed to Orestes and me
there ought to be a law against a mother
      like that.
Turns out there is: Apollo.
Apollo had us kill her.
Orestes did it, I helped. Kudos were not
      universal.
Anyway, since then Orestes fell sick.
Here he lies like something melting away.
His mother's blood comes quaking howling
      brassing bawling blacking   [30]
down his mad little veins.
Yes gods are on his case now—
those ghastly flashing goddesses I hesitate to
      name:
repeat after me, *Eumenides*!
Six days since our mother was slain and put
      in the purging fire.
Six days without food or bathing, Orestes
      huddles in his blankets.
There's the odd sane moment he sits and
      weeps,
then jumps out of bed to race up and down
      like a wild pony.

But the city of Argos declares us banned
from hearth and fire and conversation,   [40]
us matricides.
This day they will vote
to stone us or not.
We have a hope:
Menelaos arrives today from Troy with his
    ships.
He sent Helen ahead, and he sent her by
    night,
lest people see her walking in daylight—
    people
whose sons died at Troy—and go at her
    with stones.
She's in the house bemoaning her troubles.
Her one comfort now is her daughter
    Hermione,   [50]
sent here by Menelaos when he sailed to
    Troy
to be raised in our house.
This girl is Helen's joy, her way of forgetting.

So I'm watching down the road for
    Menelaos.
If he doesn't save us we're done for.
An unlucky house is an impotent thing.
    Known fact.

[*Enter* HELEN *from the house.*]

HELEN   O child of Klytaimestra and Agamemnon,
Elektra so long unwed,

you wretched girl, how are you?—you and
    your poor Orestes
who's turned out to be a mother killer,
    hasn't he?   [60]
Yet talking to you does not pollute me.
I ascribe your crime to Apollo.
Still, I bewail Klytaimestra's death. My sister.
For I sailed off to Troy, crazed by a god as
    you know,
and never saw her again.
I am bereaved. I do lament.

ELEKTRA   Helen, why should I say what you see with
    your own eyes?
We're a mess.
I sit without sleep keeping watch on a
    corpse—
to judge from his breathing he's all but
    dead—   [70]
while you, miraculously happy wife of a
    miraculously happy husband,
well, let's say you've got us on a bad day.

HELEN   How long is he lying like this?

ELEKTRA   Since the murder.

HELEN   I pity the boy. I pity the mother.

ELEKTRA   Yes well, so it goes. He's broken down.

HELEN   Listen dear, will you do me a favor?

ELEKTRA   I'm more or less occupied at the moment.

HELEN   Go to my sister's grave for me—

ELEKTRA   To my mother's grave? Why in the world?   [80]

HELEN   —and bring her offerings? Grave offerings?

ELEKTRA   Isn't that your responsibility?

HELEN   But you know, I'm ashamed to show myself
to the public eye.

ELEKTRA   Bit late for those scruples. You left the
house brazenly enough
once upon a time.

HELEN   True but unkind.

ELEKTRA   And what sort of shame is it you feel?

HELEN   The fathers of those who lie dead at Troy,
them I have reason to fear.

ELEKTRA   No kidding.

HELEN   So you'll do it?

ELEKTRA   I could not even look at my mother's grave.   [90]

HELEN   But it gives such a bad impression for a
servant to go.

ELEKTRA   Send Hermione.

HELEN   Oh quite unseemly. She's just a girl.

ELEKTRA   Think of it as compensation. My mother
           gave her a home after all.

HELEN   Good point. I'll send Hermione. Thanks.
           Hermione! Come out here, child!

           [Enter HERMIONE.*]*

HELEN   Take these offerings to Klytaimestra's
                tomb—there's honey mixed with
           milk and a dash of wine, some hair from my
                head.
           Go stand at the grave and pour them and
                say:
           "Your sister Helen sends these gifts.   [100]
           She cannot approach your tomb herself, for
                fear of the Argive mob."
           Urge her to think kindly on me, on you, on
                my husband—
           and these two poor souls ruined by god.
           Promise her whatever people give the dead
                I'll give.
           Now go. Be quick. Mind the way home.

           [Exit HELEN *into the house,* HERMIONE *by side
           entrance.]*

ELEKTRA   Helen! What a masterpiece!
            How is it some people manage to come out
                on top every time?
            Did you see how she'd trimmed just the
                very tips of her hair,
            not to spoil its beauty? Same old Helen.
            May the gods hate you! You wrecked me,   [110]
            you wrecked a whole generation of Greeks!
            Ah, here come my friends to share my
                sorrows.
            They might wake Orestes—how I dread to
                see him stirred into panic
            again!
            Dear ladies, go softly, don't make any sound.
            Your kindness is welcome but once he
                wakes up it's agony.

CHORUS   Silently, silently, lighten the foot, hush the
                                        sound.

ELEKTRA   Steer clear of the bed, go this way round.

CHORUS   This way round.

ELEKTRA   Sh, sh, make your voice as a breath through
                                a reed.   [120]

CHORUS   Softly indeed.

ELEKTRA   So softly proceed.
                    Now why have you come?
            It's a long while Orestes is lying undone.

CHORUS   How is he doing, if you can say?

ELEKTRA   He is breathing still but he groans all day.

CHORUS   Poor creature!

ELEKTRA   Don't waken the sleeper!

CHORUS   Poor victim of acts sent by god!

ELEKTRA   Wrong were the acts, wrong was the god!   [130]
But if you murder your mother, what are
the odds?

CHORUS   Look he is moving!

ELEKTRA   Can't you stop shouting?

CHORUS   No, he's still at rest.

ELEKTRA   Go home now, it's best.

CHORUS   He sleeps on unaware.

ELEKTRA   Still let us take care.
O Lady Night!
you who give sleep to mortals when they
are broken by toil
come from the dark, come on your wings,   [140]
for we are a substance beginning to spoil.
Agamemnon's house is in despair.
Ah!—the sound—stay back from his bed,

stay away from his poor sleeping head!
Dear friends, I pray, beware!

CHORUS   Where does the end of his suffering lie?

ELEKTRA   Of course he'll die.
As he takes no food, I see no other.

CHORUS   Clearly, no other.

ELEKTRA   Apollo made us sacrificial victims   [150]
in his murder exchange of father for mother.

CHORUS   Justice, on the one hand.

ELEKTRA   Evil, on the other.
Mother, as you killed so you die.
But you've ruined us all.
You at least went off to be among the dead.
I live on here as corpse beside Orestes' bed.
Nights and tears and groaning, nothing else
is mine.
No marriage, no house, no children, just
time.

CHORUS   Elektra, here, your brother's coming round.   [160]
But I don't like the look of him.

ORESTES   O beautiful motions of sleep how sweetly
you came to me,
O Lady Oblivion how kindly you clear
away pain.

Where am I? How did I get here? I've no
idea. My mind is gone.

ELEKTRA   Dear one. Bless your sleep.
Shall I touch you, help you?

ORESTES   Yes, oh yes. Wipe the foam from my mouth
and my eyes.

ELEKTRA   To serve you is sweet. I am your sister.

ORESTES   Support my side. Move the hair off my face,
I can barely see.

ELEKTRA   Your poor unwashed hair, it's gone all wild.   [170]

ORESTES   Lay me back down. When the madness
leaves I'm limp as a girl.

ELEKTRA   There you go, down on your sickbed again.

ORESTES   Set me back upright, swivel me round—
there's no pleasing the sick!
I hate being helpless.

ELEKTRA   Do you want to try putting your feet on the
ground? It's been so long.
But change is sweet.

ORESTES   Yes by all means. That will seem like good
health.
And seeming is better than nothing.

ELEKTRA   Listen, dear brother, now while the Furies
            are letting you think straight.

ORESTES   You have some news? I hope it's good. I
            have enough trouble.   [180]

ELEKTRA   Menelaos is here, he and his ships.

ORESTES   Come to save us? He certainly does owe a
            debt to our father.

ELEKTRA   Bringing Helen home from Troy.

ORESTES   Better if he'd come back alone.
            That woman is trouble.

ELEKTRA   All the women of that family are trouble.

ORESTES   Well, make up your mind to be different.
            You can, you know.

ELEKTRA   What's wrong with your eyes? You're
            slipping away again!

ORESTES   O Mother I beg you—don't send the
            snakes! Don't send
            the bloodyfaced women down on me!—ah
            they are here!

ELEKTRA   Stay quiet, poor mad one, there's nothing
            there.   [190]

ORESTES   Apollo! Here they come like killer dogs,
           goddesses hot with the glow of hell!

ELEKTRA   I'll hold on to you, I'll keep you still.
           You're going into convulsions.

ORESTES   Let me be! You Fury! You're one of them!
           You grip my waist to hurl me into hell!

ELEKTRA   Misery! Who can help? We're fighting the
              supernatural!

ORESTES   Give me the bow, Apollo's gift.
           He said to use it when these creatures come
              to ravage my mind.
           I'll shoot them down, gods or not.   [200]
           Hear those arrows whiz through the air?
              Ah! Ah!
           What are you waiting for, bloodsucking
              women, go! Away!
           Apollo's to blame, not me!
           Oh.
           Oh what.
           Oh what am I doing. What am I doing
              raving like this.
           I cannot breathe!
           Where am I? How did I get out of bed?
           Now again I see calm water, the storm sinks
              away.
           Sister, why do you weep and hide your
              head?   [210]

You make me ashamed! I am an impossible
    burden, aren't I.
Poor girl, don't melt yourself for my sake.
It's true you gave your approval but the deed
    was mine,
the mother blood is mine. I blame Apollo.
He put me up to it. Now where is he?
And I wonder what my father would say if
    he were here.
Would he have tried to stop me killing her?
I think he would, I fear he would.
Uncover your head, dear one, stay your
    tears.
No doubt we are in a bad situation.   [220]
But if you give me comfort when I get
    hopeless
I'll do the same for you.
Now go into the house, take sleep, take
    food and wash yourself.
If you fall sick too we're truly lost.
All we have is us.

ELEKTRA All we have is impossible.
To live or die with you—it comes to the
    same thing for me anyway.
Without you what am I? Brotherless
    fatherless friendless.
All the same, I'll do what you say—
but you lie down and stay quiet.   [230]
Don't let the panic in.
Even imaginary demons can drive you to
    despair.

[Exit ELEKTRA *into the house.]*

CHORUS   AIAI!
O racing raging goddesses!
You dance a dance that is no dance
screaming
down the sky
in search of justice,
bowling down the sky in search of blood!
Eumenides! I pray you off, I pray you out!   [240]
Let Agamemnon's son
forget the lunacy
that drives him terribly about!
Alas for the deeds you did, boy, alas for the
ruin you meet—
all because Apollo barked out an oracle
from his legendary Delphic seat!

O Zeus,
what pity, what ordeal
comes drumming the poor boy down
so tears on tears   [250]
combine for him
and some avenger
channels his mother's blood into the house
to drive him wild? I cry down grief, I cry
down grief!
Good fortune does not last for men.
Some god flips up the sail
and blasts the boat against a ruin reef.
Still we celebrate the house of godborn

Tantalos—
what else
could possibly make sense to us?   [260]

[Enter MENELAOS *from a side entrance.]*

MENELAOS   O house! How glad I am to look on you—
now I'm
back from Troy—at the same time I grieve.
No hearth more wrapped in wretchedness
than this.
I learned of Agamemnon's death
when I was coasting Malea.
Out of the waves the prophet Glaukos
spoke to me
(he is a god who does not lie).
"Menelaos," he said, "your brother lies
dead.
He's had his last bath at the hands of his
wife."
We wept, my sailors and I.   [270]
Then I put in at Nauplia and sent my wife
ahead,
thinking to come and embrace Orestes and
his mother.
I assumed they were well. Then a sailor told
me
of Klytaimestra's unholy end.
Now tell me, where is he—
Agamemnon's child who had it in him to
do this dread thing?

He was a babe in her arms when I left for
    Troy.
I might not recognize him now.

ORESTES   Here is Orestes. I'm the one you want.
I'll tell you all about my sufferings. Gladly.   [280]
But first, your knees I clasp
as suppliant. I pray to you.
Save me! You've arrived in the nick of time.

MENELAOS   Gods! What do I see? Which of the dead is
    this?

ORESTES   Well said. I might as well be dead.

MENELAOS   You look like a wild animal. You poor
    man.

ORESTES   It's my deeds not my looks that shame me.

MENELAOS   Your eyes are terrible.

ORESTES   Forget the body. I still have my name.

MENELAOS   I really hadn't expected to find you in this
    condition.   [290]

ORESTES   Mother murderer. Yes that's me.

MENELAOS   So I hear. Don't dwell on it.

ORESTES   Some evil spirit is dwelling on me.

MENELAOS   What's wrong with you? What sickness
            wastes you away?

ORESTES   Conscience. I know what I've done.

MENELAOS   How do you mean?

ORESTES   Grief is killing me.

MENELAOS   She is a dread goddess. But curable.

ORESTES   And fits of madness. Mother madness.
            Mother blood.

MENELAOS   When did that start?   [300]

ORESTES   The day I built her tomb.

MENELAOS   Was it at home or near the pyre?

ORESTES   At night as I waited to take up the bones.

MENELAOS   Who else was there?

ORESTES   Pylades, my accomplice in murder.

MENELAOS   What sort of visions plague you?

ORESTES   Three females who look like Night.

MENELAOS   I know who you mean. I don't want to
            name them.

ORESTES   You're right, they have power.

MENELAOS   And they are the ones dancing you on to
            madness?   [310]

ORESTES   Oh dance me they do.

MENELAOS   Yet it's not surprising, given your crime.

ORESTES   But I have one escape.

MENELAOS   Don't say death, that would be stupid.

ORESTES   No, I mean Apollo, who assigned me to kill
            my mother.

MENELAOS   A somewhat inept divinity.

ORESTES   We are slaves to the gods. Whatever gods
            are.

MENELAOS   Yet Apollo does not help you?

ORESTES   He bides his time. That is gods' way.

MENELAOS   How long dead is your mother?   [320]

ORESTES   This is the sixth day. Her pyre still warm.

MENELAOS   So *some* gods are quick—the mother
            avengers.

ORESTES   Inept or not, Apollo will come through
           for me.

MENELAOS   And how do you stand with the town?

ORESTES   So despised no one will talk to me.

MENELAOS   Have you not purified your hands of blood
           in the conventional way?

ORESTES   No, I am shut out of houses wherever I go.

MENELAOS   Are there certain men trying to drive you
           out of the town?

ORESTES   Oiax—he hates my father because of some
           incident at Troy.

MENELAOS   Ah yes, the death of Palamedes.   [330]

ORESTES   In which I had no part.

MENELAOS   Who else is against you? Aigisthos? His
           people?

ORESTES   Yes they abuse me. And they run the town.

MENELAOS   You're not allowed to hold Agamemnon's
           scepter?

ORESTES   I'm not allowed to live!

MENELAOS   Give me details.

ORESTES   Today they will vote.

MENELAOS   Vote on what? Your exile?

ORESTES   Death by stoning.

MENELAOS   Why haven't you fled?   [340]

ORESTES   I am surrounded.

MENELAOS   By whom?

ORESTES   Long story short, the whole citizen body.

MENELAOS   Oh you poor man. Complete catastrophe.

ORESTES   To you my hopes run. You are my escape.
            You've come at a time when your fortunes
                are high
            and ours are not. Help us. We are your kin.
            You owe our father, you know that.
            Don't be one of those friends in name
                only.

CHORUS   Here comes Tyndareus, old and struggling.   [350]
            He's dressed in black, in mourning for his
                daughter.

            [Enter TYNDAREUS.]

ORESTES   I'm lost, Menelaos. Here comes Tyndareus.
        Before him I am utterly
ashamed.
Why, he used to carry me in his arms when
        I was a baby—
he and his wife, they treasured me. I've
        repaid them badly.
What darkness can I find to hide me from
        his eyes?

TYNDAREUS   Where is he, where is Menelaos? My
        daughter's husband.
I was pouring libation on Klytaimestra's
        grave
when I heard he'd arrived with his wife.
Safe after so many years!   [360]
Take me to him. I want to shake his right
        hand.

MENELAOS   Joy to you, old man.

TYNDAREUS   And to you, my son-in-law—EA!—
here is the mother killer snaking about
        in front of the house!
Look at him, look how he drips unhealth—
        shudder object!

MENELAOS   He is the son of my beloved brother.

TYNDAREUS   You mean to say he is anything like his
        father?

MENELAOS   He is. But very, very unfortunate. And I
            have obligations toward him.

TYNDAREUS   Your time in the East has barbarized you.

MENELAOS   It was always Greek to respect one's kin.   [370]

TYNDAREUS   And also to respect the laws.

MENELAOS   But not to make oneself a slave of necessity.

TYNDAREUS   Well, that's your doctrine. I reject it.

MENELAOS   You've got testy in old age. You used to be
            smarter.

TYNDAREUS   What does *smart* have to do with this?
            You call him *smart*?
            A man who doesn't know the difference
                between right and wrong?
            Who ignores justice and flouts Greek law?
            When Agamemnon breathed his last, struck
                down by my daughter—
            oh I agree, a despicable deed—   [380]
            what Orestes ought to have done, what was
                right and proper,
            was throw her out of the house.
            Proper, righteous, within the law.
            But as things are now, he's taken on board
                the same devils as she.
            He was right to think her evil
            but this murder makes him more to blame.

Listen, I have one question for you,
    Menelaos.
Suppose one day Orestes' wife should kill
    Orestes
and then Orestes' son murder his mother in
    revenge.
And then *his* son pay off that murder with
    another one—   [390]
where will it end?
Our forefathers thought all this through.
When a man got blood on his hands
they had him banished. Not murdered.
Otherwise blood pollution goes on hand to
    hand forever.
Now me I despise impure women—
in the first place my daughter who slew her
    husband
(and this Helen of yours I won't even
    mention!
You launched a thousand ships for *that*?)
but the law I'll defend as far as I can.   [400]
All this killing, it's like animals.
How can civilization survive?

I mean *[to* ORESTES*]* what did you feel, you
    shameless creature,
when your mother bared her breast and
    begged you for pity?
I weep to think of it.
At any rate it's obvious the gods hate you—
you're paying off your mother's blood in
    bouts of lunacy.

Who needs more evidence?
So my point is, Menelaos, don't go against
    the gods,
don't choose to help this one.   [410]
Let the townspeople stone him to death.
My daughter paid her price by dying.
Yet it was not right she die by *his* hand.
I'm a fortunate man in other ways but not
    in daughters.
There I struck out.

CHORUS   Lucky the man who gets good children.
          What a lottery.

ORESTES   I'm afraid to say anything to you, old man.
          Whatever I say will offend you
          and your great age makes me hesitate.   [420]
          Well, here goes.
          I am unholy. A mother killer.
          At the same time pious and lawful. A father
              avenger.
          It's a contradiction. What should I have
              done?
          My father begot me, your daughter bore me,
          as the farmland takes the seed: no father, no
              child.
          He is my origin. That was my reasoning.
          And as for your daughter—the word
              mother shames me—
          you know she had something going on the
              side. Repulsive to say this.
          Aigisthos was her secret househusband.   [430]

I killed him and made sacrifice of her.

Unholy yes. But I gave justice to my father.

As for your wish to see me stoned,

listen, I am a benefactor of Greece!

Picture this: wanton women throughout the
    land

murdering husbands, running to sons for
    refuge,

hunting pity with bared breasts—

they'd be killing their men at the slightest
    pretext.

I put a stop to this. You call me unjust?

My hatred of her was in every way just.   [440]

She betrayed the commander in chief of the
    Greek army—

defiled his bed when he was off fighting for
    the homeland.

She knew she'd done wrong and slew my
    father lest he punish her.

Should I have kept silent? How would the
    dead man like that?

Wouldn't *his* Furies be dancing their dance
    around me now?

Or does my mother have a monopoly on
    ghastly goddesses?

As a matter of fact, isn't it all your fault for
    engendering her?

You ruined me!

Through her I lost my father and became a
    matricide.

Look, Telemachos didn't have to kill his
    mother—why?   [450]

Because she wasn't piling husband on top of
    husband.
Odysseus' marriage bed is still pure.
Anyway, the orders I followed were
    Apollo's.
Call *him* unholy! Put *him* to death!
Again I ask you, what should I have done!
Can't I call upon the god to clear this
    charge?
If not, where else can I run?
No don't say my deed was evil.
Unlucky, sad, disastrous, yes. Not evil.

CHORUS   Women always complicate things don't they.   [460]

TYNDAREUS   You're out of control.
You pain my mind, you make me burn!
I only came to tend my daughter's tomb,
now here's an extra task—
I'll go to the Argive assembly and shake
    them out against you and your sister.
By stoning *you will pay*.
That girl deserves it more than you—'twas
    she
who savaged you against your mother,
sending endless hostile tales and adverse
    dreams of Aigisthos and adultery
may the gods of hell curse that bitter bed—   [470]
it was Elektra set the house ablaze, not using
    fire.
Menelaos, I have this to say to you:
mark my hatred.

Do not help this man.
He is an enemy of gods, let him be stoned.
Here is my warning: stay out of Sparta
and don't take on criminals as friends.
Now *[to servant]* get me out of here.

[Exit TYNDAREUS.*]*

ORESTES   Good, go! I prefer talking to this man
                without you interrupting.
            Menelaos, why are you pacing in circles,
                what are your thoughts?   [480]

MENELAOS   Give me a minute, I'm pondering.
            Which way to turn. Not sure, not sure.

ORESTES   Well, don't make a snap judgment.
            Hear me out.

MENELAOS   Okay, I will.
            There are times when silence is better than
                speech,
            times when speech is better than silence.

ORESTES   And a long speech best of all.
            Here goes.
            I'm not asking you for a free gift, Menelaos,   [490]
            but to pay what you owe. What you got
                from my father.
            I don't mean money (although life is my
                most precious asset)—
            no, I am a criminal.

To balance that, I need a crime from you.
Just as my father undertook to do wrong—
    to make war on Troy—
not for his own sake but to put right the
    offense of your wife,
so you must give back a wrong for a wrong.
And he gave his body too, as friends do,
stood by your side in battle,
so you could recover your wife.   [500]
Pay this back in kind.
Stand by me for one day—I'm not asking
    ten years!
Now, he had to slaughter his daughter at
    Aulis as well,
but I let that go, you don't have to murder
    Hermione.
The fact is, you've got the upper hand here,
    not me.
So grant me my life, for my father's sake.
If I die I leave his house bereft.
You'll say "Impossible!" but that's just it.
Impossible situations are where we need
    friends.
If I had god on my side I'd be self-sufficient!   [510]

All Greeks think of you as a man who loves
    his wife
(I don't say this to be flattering)—in her
    name
I beseech you—I'm desperate!
On behalf of my house
and the blood you share with my father,

imagine him listening to this—
imagine his soul hovering near,
imagine him saying all that I say!
Okay, there you have it. I've made my
　　claim.
I want survival. Who doesn't!　　　　　　　[520]

CHORUS　I'm only a woman but I beg you too,
help those in need. You have the power.

MENELAOS　Let me be perfectly clear, Orestes, I do
　　respect you
and want to share your pain, that's what
　　family is for—
fighting enemies to the death.
So long as god gives the means.
I repeat, so long as god gives the means.
My own force is slight—I've been on the
　　road for years—
army disbanded, friends gone.
In open war we would not prevail against
　　Argos.　　　　　　　　　　　　　　　[530]
What about negotiations? There's an area of
　　hope.
Stupid to think it will be easy—
once the mob catches fire you can't just
　　stamp it out—
but with caution, diplomacy, just the right
　　timing,
we might see this storm blow itself away.
Then you walk in and ask for whatever you
　　want.

A mob lives on passion but also *compassion*.
Wait for the moment. Timing is key.
So. I'll go
try to persuade Tyndareus and his Argives   [540]
to use their zeal wisely.
You know, when the sail is too tight the
    ship goes under:
slack off a bit and it justifies itself.
God hates a fanatic. So do good citizens.
Anyway, whatever you think, I can't save
    you by main strength,
it will have to be cunning.
I'm just one lone spear.
Now granted, Argos is an unlikely place to
    try diplomacy.
But tactically speaking, what is our option?

[Exit MENELAOS.*]*

ORESTES You worm! What good are you? You'll make
    war for a woman   [550]
but not your own kin? You'll turn your back
    on me
now that Agamemnon's cause is finished?
Father, we are friendless after all!
Betrayed! No hope!
This man was my exit strategy.
Oh but look,
here comes Pylades, my dearest friend, a
    sight as sweet
as calm water to sailors.

[Enter PYLADES.*]*

PYLADES   I raced through the town as soon as I heard
                    of the citizen assembly.
                I saw it too.   [560]
                They mean to kill you and your sister.
                What's going on? How are you faring—
                    dearest, sweetest,
                best of friends—you know you are all these
                    to me.

ORESTES   Our cause is lost. I'll tell you briefly.

PYLADES   Then I'm lost too. Friends share such things.

ORESTES   Menelaos is no good.

PYLADES   Not surprising. Look at his wife.

ORESTES   No use to me at all.

PYLADES   He's actually here?

ORESTES   Yes, he's finally back. But he's just no help.   [570]

PYLADES   And has he shipped home his profligate
                    wife?

ORESTES   Oh I think *she* runs the ship.

PYLADES   Where is she, that weapon of mass
                    destruction?

ORESTES   In my house—if you can call it mine.

PYLADES   What did you ask of Menelaos?

ORESTES   To save me from stoning, me and my sister.

PYLADES   God! what did he say?

ORESTES   He got very cautious, as bad friends do.

PYLADES   On what pretext?

ORESTES   Well, Tyndareus came along.   [580]

PYLADES   In a rage about his daughter?

ORESTES   You got it. Menelaos took his side.

PYLADES   Scared to shoulder your burden?

ORESTES   Never was much of a warrior. Except with
           women.

PYLADES   It looks bad for you.

ORESTES   The citizens are casting a vote.

PYLADES   Vote?

ORESTES   Life or death.

PYLADES   Let's get out of here!

ORESTES   We're surrounded—guards on every road.   [590]

PYLADES   Yes, I noticed the streets are blocked with
          weapons.

ORESTES   Our house is beset like a town under
          siege.

PYLADES   Now ask me my story. The fact is, I'm
          ruined too.

ORESTES   How?

PYLADES   My father drove me out of the house.

ORESTES   On what charge?

PYLADES   That I joined in your mother's murder and
          am unholy.

ORESTES   O poor man! My troubles are really your
          troubles, it seems.

PYLADES   But I'm no Menelaos. I can bear this.

ORESTES   You don't fear the Argives?   [600]

PYLADES   The Argives are not my people.

ORESTES   A mob is a terrible thing when its leaders
          are corrupt.

PYLADES   But if the leaders are honest, decent
    deliberations can occur.

ORESTES   What do you say we make a joint plan?

PYLADES   Starting how?

ORESTES   Starting with me going to the Argive
    assembly to tell them—

PYLADES   that your actions were just—

ORESTES   in avenging my father—

PYLADES   and although they are eager to seize you—

ORESTES   I won't cower in silence and die—   [610]

PYLADES   that would be craven!

ORESTES   So what should I do?

PYLADES   Any chance of staying safe here?

ORESTES   No, none.

PYLADES   And if you flee?

ORESTES   Maybe, with luck.

PYLADES   Well, that's better than staying.

ORESTES   So I should go?

PYLADES   At least your death won't be dishonorable.

ORESTES   Right. I'll avoid looking like a coward—   [620]

PYLADES   more than if you stay.

ORESTES   Besides, my cause is just.

PYLADES   Pray that they see this.

ORESTES   And people might pity me—

PYLADES   after all, you are of noble blood!

ORESTES   And indignant at my father's death.

PYLADES   Obviously.

ORESTES   I must go. Unmanly to die here.

PYLADES   I agree.

ORESTES   Should I tell my sister?   [630]

PYLADES   No, for god's sake!

ORESTES   There would certainly be tears.

PYLADES   A very bad omen.

ORESTES   Surely silence is better.

PYLADES   And you'll save time.

ORESTES   One last worry—

PYLADES   What?

ORESTES   The ghastly goddesses—they'll send my wits
            astray.

PYLADES   I'll take care of you.

ORESTES   It's rotten work.   [640]

PYLADES   Not to me. Not if it's you.

ORESTES   Beware the contagion of madness.

PYLADES   Come now.

ORESTES   You won't shrink back?

PYLADES   A friend does not shrink back.

ORESTES   Then let's go.

PYLADES   Let's go.

ORESTES   Take me to my father's tomb.

PYLADES   Why?

ORESTES   So I can pray for him to save us.   [650]

PYLADES   Yes, that would be proper.

ORESTES   My mother's tomb—I will not look at.

PYLADES   No, she was your enemy.
               Okay let's hurry, in case the Argives are
                   voting.
               Lean on me.
               I'll bring you through town, through the
                   crowd,
               I see no shame in it.
               How else would I act, I am your friend!

ORESTES   There's an old saying—a good friend
               is worth ten thousand relatives.   [660]

CHORUS   Huge wealth, huge virtue, huge Greek
                                   pride
                       has turned away from happiness
                           for the house of Atreus
                           because in ancient days
                               from ancient ways
                       came strife and hideous feasting,
                           slaughter of children,
                               blood for blood
                       endlessly being paid back.

                 Atrocity disguised as good—to cut the flesh
                                   of kin   [670]
                 and show a blacksoaked sword to the sun.

Evil that calls itself virtue
is the paranoia
of men whose minds have broken down.
Klytaimestra screamed out
"Child, your act is unholy!
Don't make yourself infamous
just to gratify your father!"

What disease, what tears, what pity is worse
than mother blood on your own hands.   [680]
You did the deed
and panic struck—
the ghastly goddesses are hunting you!
They spin your eyes, they turn you inside
out!
You wretch,
your mother bared her breast, you sank your
sword in it!
Payback for the father.

[Enter ELEKTRA *from the house.]*

ELEKTRA   Ladies, has poor Orestes run from the house
                 in a frenzy?

CHORUS   Not at all. He's gone to address the Argive
                 assembly.

ELEKTRA   Oh no! Whose idea was this?   [690]

CHORUS   Pylades'. But look,
                 here's a messenger to tell us what happened.

[Enter MESSENGER *from a side entrance.]*

MESSENGER   O poor child, poor child of Agamemnon,
                    lady Elektra,
                 hear my sorry news.

ELEKTRA   We are lost!

MESSENGER   The Argives voted death for you and your
                    brother.

ELEKTRA   OIMOI! I knew this would happen.
                 But tell me how it went, what did they
                    say?
                 Do we die by sword or stoning?

MESSENGER   Well, I came in from the country for news
                    of you and Orestes   [700]
                 (I'm a poor man, you know, but your father
                    always gave me handouts)
                 and I saw a crowd gathering.
                 "What's going on?" I asked someone.
                 "Look over there," he said, "Orestes has
                    shown up for trial."
                 I looked and saw an apparition
                    approaching—
                 Pylades and your brother,
                 the one dropping and fainting with disease,
                 the other lifting him along like a little
                    brother.
                 So the assembly filled up, the question was
                    put:

Who wishes to speak on whether Orestes
    should die as a matricide?   [710]
Then rose up Talthybios, your father's old
    comrade.
But you know he's a pawn of the ruling
    regime,
so he talked double, glorifying your father,
not quite praising your brother,
interlacing fine words with foul,
alluding to laws and parents and precedent,
all the while giving a glad eye to the bosses
    at the back of the room.
That's what that breed is like: heralds always
    side with power.
Next spoke Diomedes.
He was for exile, not death, on moral
    grounds.   [720]
Some shouted assent, others objected.
Then rose up a man with no door on his
    mouth—
a big talker—guy with a talent for abuse
(and we know who hired him).
He said to kill you and Orestes by stoning.
Tyndareus seconded.
Then another stood up and spoke on the
    opposite side.
A manly man, decent, a farmer but
    intelligent.
He tried to come to grips with the
    arguments.
Said we should crown Orestes for avenging
    his father   [730]

and putting a godless woman to death.
She was a threat to our whole way of life, he
    said.
How could we go off to war
with wives like that at home, defiling the
    master's bed!
Respectable people found this fellow
    convincing.
No one else spoke.
Your brother came forward.
Argives, he said, no less than my father
was I fighting for you
when I killed her.   [740]
If murder of husbands is granted to women
who'll escape death? Should we be their
    slaves?
It's all upside down! *She* was the criminal!
If you put me to death, where are our laws?
    Anarchy's next!
Well, he didn't persuade the majority,
though some of us thought he made sense.
That other scoundrel won the day.
The vote was for death.
Orestes just barely persuaded the crowd to
    give up the stoning idea.
Said he would die by his own hand,   [750]
this day, with you.
Pylades is bringing him here now,
they're both in tears, you'll see. Bitter
    spectacle.
So get your sword ready.
Or rope, however you wish to die.

Your noble birth has been no help to you—
not to say
Apollo on his famous oracle seat!

CHORUS   I begin the lament.
I scratch my cheek
to bloody detriment,   [760]
I beat my head
and the sound echoes down to hell.
Let all the land cry out
and shave its head for grief.
Pity comes forward
for those who will die.
There are no more heroes in Greece!
Ruined and gone
is the whole house of Pelops.
Blessedness has flown.   [770]
Envy came down from gods
and a bloody vote from citizens.
O you human beings made of tears,
look how your fate goes astray from your
hopes.
Grief upon grief,
the life of mortals is a line no ruler can
draw.

ELEKTRA   I want to fly!
To the middle of the sky
where (they say) is a rock that swings on a
golden chain—
I will cry aloud   [780]
to ancient Tantalos

who fathered generations of ruin,
generations of pure pain.
You know of the horses that ran mad and
crashed in the sea.
You know the prodigies, curses, strife from
which we have never been free.
Death breeding death out of death is the
law of our house.
It all comes down on me.

CHORUS   Here comes Orestes, a man sentenced to
death
and trusty Pylades, as good as a brother,
guiding him along.

[Enter ORESTES *and* PYLADES.*]*

ELEKTRA Oh sorrow! I groan to see you standing,
brother,   [790]
at the very gates of death.
I may be looking on you for the last time!
I may be losing my mind!

ORESTES Quiet now. No female shrieking.
It is a sad business, but still.

ELEKTRA Quiet! How should I be quiet!
This may be the final daylight you and I will
ever see!

ORESTES Don't drag me down.
I'm already down! Let it be!

ELEKTRA   I feel such pity for you, for your boyhood,
          for your poor young life cut off at the roots.

ORESTES   For gods' sake don't unman me.
          I forbid you to bring me to tears.

ELEKTRA   We're about to die. I cannot not groan.
          To love life is a pitiful thing but all mortals
              do.

ORESTES   This day is ordained for us.
          We must use either rope or sword.

ELEKTRA   *You* kill me, Orestes. Don't let some Argive
              stranger
          insult Agamemnon's child.

ORESTES   No, mother blood is enough for me, I can't
              kill you.
          It must be your own hand. In your own
              way.

ELEKTRA   So be it. Sword, then.
          But I need to put my arms around your
              neck.

ORESTES   Take your pleasure. If it is pleasure.

ELEKTRA   O most beloved! We share one soul!

ORESTES   You will melt me. I want to embrace you
              too—oh why not?

Beloved sister of mine!
This takes the place of marriage and
   children for both of us, doesn't it.

ELEKTRA   PHEU! I wish we could die by the same
   sword
and lie in the same tomb.   [820]

ORESTES   That would be sweet. But we're short of
   friends to arrange this.

ELEKTRA   So Menelaos did not speak up to save your
   life, that perfidious coward?

ORESTES   Didn't show his face. He's a man with an
   eye on the throne.
Now come,
let's make a death worthy of Agamemnon.
I'll show this city I'm noble—I'll stab right
   through my liver.
And you, Elektra, match me in courage.
Pylades, be our referee.
Lay us out after death
and bury us in our father's tomb.   [830]
Farewell. I go to it.

PYLADES   Hold on, hold on, I have to protest.
Do you think I would choose to live
   without you?

ORESTES   Oh but you can't die too!

PYLADES   Why not?

ORESTES   You didn't kill your mother.

PYLADES   I shared the deed.

ORESTES   No, don't do it! You have a city, a house, a
                father, a fortune—
            I've none of these.
            It's true you can't marry my sister as I once
                promised   [840]
            but you'll find someone else. Have children,
                a life.
            Our connection is ended. Beloved
                comrade, farewell.
            She and I are finished, but you—may you
                fare and be well.

PYLADES   Oh you're way off target. I would never
                desert you—
            may the ground not accept my blood when
                I die,
            nor the bright air my soul, if I am lying.
            No, I joined in the murder, I do not plead
                innocence,
            I plotted it by your side.
            So I join you in death—you, me and this girl
            I did agree to marry her after all.   [850]
            And what would I have to say for myself in
                later life
            if I stopped being your friend the minute
                you got into trouble?

No.
We're going to die together, so let's confer:
How can we make sure Menelaos suffers
    too?

ORESTES   You genius friend, how I would love to see
    that!

PYLADES   Well, listen up.

ORESTES   I'm listening. I do want revenge.

PYLADES   Are these women trustworthy?

ORESTES   Yes they are friends.   [860]

PYLADES   How about we murder Helen? That would
    cause Menelaos pain.

ORESTES   How? I'm ready.

PYLADES   Cut her throat. Is she inside your house?

ORESTES   Yes. She's made it her own.

PYLADES   Not anymore. She's the bride of death now.

ORESTES   But how? She has slaves.

PYLADES   What sort of slaves? Mere Trojans don't
    scare me.

ORESTES   The sort who look after mirrors and
            perfumes.

PYLADES   You mean she's come *here* with all the
            luxuries of Troy?

ORESTES   I guess she finds culture in Greece a bit thin.   [870]

PYLADES   Well, free men against slaves, that's no
            problem.

ORESTES   I'd gladly die for this!

PYLADES   Likewise! I'll avenge you!

ORESTES   Explain your plan.

PYLADES   We go into the house pretending we're
            going to kill ourselves.

ORESTES   Okay.

PYLADES   We moan to Helen about our troubles.

ORESTES   Bring tears to her eyes—though she'll be
            laughing on the inside.

PYLADES   Exactly.

ORESTES   Then what?   [880]

PYLADES   We'll have swords ready under our clothing.

ORESTES   What about the slaves?

PYLADES   Lock them in another room.

ORESTES   Kill the ones who make noise.

PYLADES   After that it's obvious.

ORESTES   Death for Helen.

PYLADES   You got it. Because, here's my reasoning:
           if we were assassinating someone respectable
               it would be different.
           But all Greeks want this whore taken out.
               She's virtually a mass murderer.
           They'll call us heroes! No more "matricide"
               label for you.   [890]
           And it must not happen, it simply must not
               happen
           that Menelaos prospers from all this while
               you, your sister,
           your mother—well, I won't go there.
           Or that Menelaos has your house when it
               was Agamemnon
           got his wife back for him!
           God, how I long to put my sword through
               her throat!
           But if we're somehow foiled
           we'll set fire to these buildings before we
               die.
           Go out in a blaze of glory, safe or sorry!

CHORUS   She's a disgrace to her sex that Helen.   [900]

ORESTES Nothing is better than a genuine friend!
         Not wealth, not power, there is simply no
              equivalent.
         First you help me against Aigisthos, stand by
              me in danger,
         then you offer me revenge on my
              enemies—you're brilliant!
         But I won't go on praising, I know it gets
              onerous.
         I'll be breathing out my life here soon, I
              want to do my enemies down,
         repay their treachery, make them groan.
         I am Agamemnon's son. He ruled Greece by
              merit,
         not royal succession. And got strength from
              god.
         I will not shame him with a slave's death.   [910]
         No, I'll die free. And punish Menelaos.
         Of course what I'd like is to kill without
              having to die.
         That would be ideal. I'll make that my
              prayer.
         Doesn't cost anything to fantasize.

ELEKTRA I agree.
         Salvation for us all would be ideal.

ORESTES But how?

ELEKTRA Listen—[to PYLADES] you too.

ORESTES   Go on.

ELEKTRA   You know Helen's daughter?   [920]

ORESTES   Hermione, yes. My mother raised her.

ELEKTRA   She's gone with grave offerings on Helen's
           behalf.

ORESTES   So?

ELEKTRA   Take her hostage on her way back.

ORESTES   How will that save us?

ELEKTRA   When Helen's dead and Menelaos tries to
               do anything
           to you or me, tell him you'll kill Hermione.
           Hold a sword at her throat.
           If he complies, if he's willing to save you,
           give the girl back.   [930]
           If he blusters,
           graze her throat with the sword.
           I think he'll come round. He's no tough
               guy.
           End of speech.

ORESTES   Elektra, you think like a man!
           You deserve to live not die.
           What a wife you have lost in her, Pylades—
           or maybe not, if we survive!

PYLADES   If only that could happen!
            I'd bring her back to my hometown—big
                wedding,   [940]
            wedding songs, the whole thing.

ORESTES   But how soon will Hermione return here?
            Your plan is excellent, provided we actually
                intercept her precious little self.

ELEKTRA   She should arrive anytime now.

ORESTES   Good, then you wait for her in front of the
                house, Elektra.
            Keep watch in case anyone else shows up
                before we're finished killing—
            some uncle or ally of her father—
            let us know: bang on the door or send word
                in.
            As for us—into the house for the final test!
            Pylades, let's get our swords.   [950]
            [Turning away.] O Father who dwells in the
                house of Night
            I call upon you, Orestes your son, I call you
                to come as my ally.

ELEKTRA   Yes Father, come to us. If you hear us. Your
                children invoke you.
            We are about to die for your sake.

PYLADES   Agamemnon, kinsman of my father, hear
                my prayers.
            Save your children.

ORESTES   I killed my mother—

ELEKTRA   I touched his sword—

PYLADES   I urged him on, released him from fear.

ORESTES   We stood in your defense, Father—   [960]

ELEKTRA   we did not betray you!

PYLADES   Hearing these claims will you not save your
       children?

ORESTES   With my tears I pour you libation.

ELEKTRA   And I with my laments.

PYLADES   Enough! It's time to get on with the work.
       If cries do penetrate the ground, he hears.
       Zeus and Justice, grant us victory!
       Three friends, one trial, one righteousness.
       Either to live or to die!

       [Exit ORESTES *and* PYLADES.*]*

ELEKTRA   Dear women of Argos—   [970]

CHORUS   Yes, lady.

ELEKTRA   Stand you some by the road, some on the
         path by the house.
         Keep watch for us.

CHORUS   Watch for what?

ELEKTRA   Lest someone come along in the midst of
                     the bloodshed.

CHORUS A   Go, hurry, I'll guard this path facing east.

CHORUS B   And I this road facing west.

ELEKTRA   Swivel your eyes from this side to that.

CHORUS   We watch as you tell us.

ELEKTRA   Try to see everything.   [980]

CHORUS A   Who's that on the path? Some farmer
                        comes near!

ELEKTRA   We're lost! He'll see us!

CHORUS A   Calm down, dear, he's gone. The path is
                           empty.

ELEKTRA   [Turning.] What about your side? Is it still
                           clear?

CHORUS B   All's well here.

CHORUS A   Same on this side. No one coming.

ELEKTRA   I'll put my ear to the door.
                     You in there, why so slow?

Get on with killing!
Ha, they're not listening. Ruin!   [990]
Faced with her beauty, do their swords go
dull?
Soon some Argive will come racing to the
rescue.
Take a better look now! No time to sit still!
You go this way, you go that.

CHORUS   We're watching in every direction.

              [*Cry from within.*] O Argos, I am being
              murdered!

ELEKTRA   Hear that? The men are putting their hands
              in blood.

CHORUS   Sounds like Helen screaming.

ELEKTRA   O unfailing force of Zeus,
              come as our ally!   [1000]

              [*Cry from within.*] Menelaos, I am dying!
              Why aren't you here?

ELEKTRA   Strike her, slaughter her, ruin her, finish her
                    off!
              Slash with the two-edged sword
              that
              father-forsaking husband-forsaking
              cause of death
              cause of tears

for so many good Greek men on the banks
    of the river of Troy!

CHORUS   Quiet, quiet, I hear the sound of someone
    coming near the house.

ELEKTRA   Dear women, here is Hermione   [1010]
into the midst of murder. Let's stop
    shouting.
She is going to walk straight into the net.
A fine catch, if we catch her!
Take up your stations, keep your face calm.
I'll have my eyes cast down
as though I've no idea what's happening.
Hermione, have you come from
    Klytaimestra's grave?
Have you poured your libations?

HERMIONE   Yes, I've received her blessing.
But I'm anxious—I heard an outcry from
    the house   [1020]
when I was quite far off.

ELEKTRA   Really? An outcry? Well, our situation
    deserves outcry.

HERMIONE   Do you have some news?

ELEKTRA   Death is decreed for Orestes and me.

HERMIONE   God forbid—you are my kin!

ELEKTRA   It is fixed. We stand in the yoke of necessity.

HERMIONE   Was that the reason for the shouting in the
            house?

ELEKTRA   Yes, he fell at Helen's knees in supplication.

HERMIONE   Who?

ELEKTRA   Poor Orestes.   [1030]

HERMIONE   No wonder the house resounds.

ELEKTRA   Yes, no wonder. But won't you come and
            join our supplication
            to your mother? Menelaos is ready to kill
            us!

HERMIONE   Indeed I will come.
            May you be saved insofar as it rests with me.

            [*Exit* HERMIONE *almost.*]

HERMIONE   Who is this?

ELEKTRA   Silence!
            Salvation is here for us not you.
            Take her, take her, put the sword to her
            throat and hold it there!
            So Menelaos knows he's dealing with men,
            not Trojan toyboys!   [1040]

CHORUS   IO! IO! Women!
Stamp your feet, raise a song, cover the
sounds in the house!
Lest the Argives run to help
before I see, before I truly see
Helen lying in her own blood
or hear it from an eyewitness!
I know part of what happened, the rest is
not clear.
I know Justice came down from the gods
against Helen—
Helen who filled all Greece with tears
for the sake of that ruinous Paris   [1050]
and dragged the Greeks to Troy!

What's that sound?
One of her Trojan entourage is coming out.

[Enter TROJAN SLAVE.]

SLAVE   I escaped from death, I escaped from
doom—
in my own dear little slippers
I fled that room! O sisters!
which way can I fly
to the sea or the sky
or a big dark underground hole
to save my own dear little soul!   [1060]

CHORUS   What are you saying, you barbarian flunky,
what's going on?

SLAVE   Alas! Alas! My city is gone!
                         Scraps of it remain not one!
                         Alas for Troy! Alas for me!
                       You know it's quite unique to be
                     subject to so immoderate a catastrophe!
                     And my dear little song will make you see
                            Helen's to blame!
                            Helen's your shame!   [1070]
                      That venge-kitty poison-pretty whore!
                            Alas alas woe!

CHORUS   Can you just tell me what's happening
           inside?

SLAVE   Where I come from people say *bad shit
                                happening*
                           when they mean death.
                      Another quaint barbarian idiom is *real bad
                               shit happening*—
                        that covers blood on the floors
                        and a houseful of swords.
                            Let's cut to the wail.
                            You want some detail.   [1080]
                      Two Greek lions came into the house
                    one an army brat the other street sharp
                            but quiet as a mouse.
                     Him I did not trust—snake eyes, you know?
                    So all in tears, all humble, crouching low
                     they come toward Helen from different
                                angles.
                       Meanwhile her bodyguards are busy
                        rearranging their bangles—

they can't figure whether or not it's a trick
(your average bodyguard's not too quick).

CHORUS Where are you at this point?   [1090]

SLAVE Well girls, as it happens, I'm wafting a breeze
past her ladyship's knees
and cooling her cheek with a big Trojan
feather,
while she works her fingers off at the loom
making crimson cloth for Klytaimestra's
tomb.
Then Orestes calls to her saying, "Helen
dear,
put down your weaving and come over
here."
He leads her, he leads her, she follows away
and then it gets worse, Helen's bad day.
The snaky guy jumps on the bodyguards   [1100]
snarling out his lips,
"You Trojan trash, I'll clip your tips!"
He shoves us into cupboards, locks up the
links.
Poor us, we were helpless! but we spy
through the chinks.

CHORUS What next?

SLAVE   Horror! Mayhem! Terrible! Alas!
Bloodiness, lawlessness, evils came to pass!
What I saw, what I saw, in the house of my
lords—

from out their own shadows those two pull
their swords,
one from one side, the other from the
other,   [1110]
like wild mountain boars rushing out from
cover,
they stand facing the woman saying, *"You
die!*
Your weak husband is why:
he betrayed his own kin unto death."
She cries out *"Woe!"* and gasps for breath.
Then claps her white arms over her face
to beat a retreat out of that place.
But Orestes flings his hand in her hair
and yanks her back from going anywhere,
ready to strike his sword into her deep—   [1120]

CHORUS   So where are you and the guards, asleep?

SLAVE   The doorposts we crack with crowbars and
a yell
and run out into the room pell-mell,
stones and slings and swords in hand
but Pylades comes at us like a monster man.
Then we join swords and things get
embarrassing
(we're no match for Greeks at military
harassing)—
some fled, some dead, some begging for
their lives
and amidst all this Hermione arrives!
They lunge at her, yelling,   [1130]

then remember Helen—
who at that very moment simply vanishes
from sight!
O Zeus! O Light! O Dark of Night!
I know not how!
Truth is, at that point I made my bow.
Panicked a bit, took to my heels.
You know how it feels.

CHORUS   The weirdness goes on. It just goes on.
Here's Orestes. Got his sword out. Looks
pretty excited.

[Enter ORESTES*.]*

ORESTES   Where is that man who ran out of the
house?   [1140]

SLAVE   I bow before you, King, right to the ground
in barbarian style.

ORESTES   This isn't Troy, we're in Argos.

SLAVE   Everywhere is a sweet place to escape death.

ORESTES   Have you been shouting for help for
Menelaos?

SLAVE   No, no, no—help for you! I'm on your side!

ORESTES   So it was right and just that Helen perish?

SLAVE   Right and just three times over.

ORESTES   Your tongue wants to gratify. You don't
             really believe that.

SLAVE   Don't believe Helen screwed Greece as well
             as Troy? *Please.*

ORESTES   Swear you do, or I'll kill you.   [1150]

SLAVE   I swear on my life! Is that convincing?

ORESTES   Was it like this at Troy—you Trojans all
             cringing in fear?

SLAVE   Please remove your blade from my throat. I
             don't like the glare.

ORESTES   Afraid of turning to stone? Like people who
             see the Gorgon?

SLAVE   Afraid of turning to corpse. What's a
             Gorgon?

ORESTES   Interesting, even a slave fears death—yet you
             could escape misery!

SLAVE   Every man, slave or free, loves to look upon
             the light.

ORESTES   Very poetic. Your eloquence has saved you.
             Go indoors.

SLAVE   You won't kill me?

ORESTES   Go.   [1160]

SLAVE   Fabulous.

ORESTES   Unless I reconsider.

SLAVE   Not fabulous.

ORESTES   Oh you idiot, I can't be bothered cutting
          the throat of a eunuch.
          I only came out to stop you setting up a hue
          and cry.
          But I'm not afraid to fight Menelaos!
          Bring him on, with his big blond hair and
          fancy looks!
          If he leads the Argives against me
          he'll find two dead bodies, his wife and his
          daughter both.

          [Exit TROJAN SLAVE *into the house.]*

CHORUS   Look how things fall!   [1170]
          Into agony, into another agony the house
                          plunges
              dreadful and deep for the children of
                          Atreus.
          What should we do—take the news to the
                          town?
          Or keep silence—that's safer isn't it?

Look at the housefront how it dissolves—
   smoke rising high in the air.
They are lighting the torches, setting the fire
   and they do not shrink back though the
      work is dire!
But some god controls all human outcomes.
   And vengeance is an overwhelming force.   [1180]
   This house is finished.

Here comes Menelaos on sharp feet.
He must have heard what is happening.
Bolt the doors, Orestes. You've got the
   upper hand now!

[Enter MENELAOS *from a side entrance.]*

MENELAOS   I hear drastic deeds have been done by those
      two lions—
   they aren't human beings!
   That my wife is not dead but vanished away.
   Some silly rumor. Some tactic of Orestes'.
   Ludicrous.
   Open the doors!   [1190]
   I'll rescue my daughter at least from
      murdering hands.

[Enter ORESTES *onto the roof of the house with*
PYLADES *and* HERMIONE.*]*

ORESTES   Don't touch those doors!
   You there, Menelaos—you of the towering
      indignation, yes I mean you!—

or I'll smash your skull with a copingstone.
The doors are bolted fast. You're not
rescuing anyone.

MENELAOS   EA! What's this! I see torches blazing,
people looming on the roof and there's my
daughter with a sword at her throat!

ORESTES   Do you want to ask questions or listen to
me?

MENELAOS   Neither. But I guess I better listen.

ORESTES   It may interest you that I plan to kill your
daughter.   [1200]

MENELAOS   And you've already killed Helen?

ORESTES   I *wish*. No, the gods snatched her away.

MENELAOS   You mock me!

ORESTES   Unfortunately not. In fact I heartily
regret—

MENELAOS   Regret what?

ORESTES   I didn't knock that unclean thing all the
way to hell.

MENELAOS   Your mother's blood wasn't enough for you?

ORESTES   I could never tire of killing evil women.

MENELAOS   Return my wife's body so I can bury it.

ORESTES   Petition the gods. Meanwhile I'll go ahead
           with your daughter.   [1210]

MENELAOS   The mother killer seeks to pile murder on
           murder!

ORESTES   The defender of a father, whom you
           betrayed to his death.

MENELAOS   And you, Pylades, you're part of this too?

ORESTES   Yes he is.

MENELAOS   And how will you get away? Intend to
           sprout wings?

ORESTES   We won't be leaving. We're going to set the
           house on fire.

MENELAOS   Lay waste your own ancestral home?

ORESTES   So you can't have it. And I'll slaughter your
           girl over the flames.

MENELAOS   Go ahead, kill her. I'll get my revenge.

ORESTES   So be it.   [1220]

MENELAOS   *No don't do it!*

ORESTES   Oh be quiet. Endure what you deserve.

MENELAOS   And what do you deserve? To go on living?

ORESTES   Yes. And rule this land.

MENELAOS   Which land?

ORESTES   Argos.

MENELAOS   Oh that would be dandy wouldn't it, to
                      have you touching sacred vessels!

ORESTES   Why not?

MENELAOS   And dispatching holy victims!

ORESTES   Whereas you'd be more suitable?   [1230]

MENELAOS   My hands are clean.

ORESTES   Your mind is not.

MENELAOS   But who would want to have anything to
                      do with you?

ORESTES   Anyone who loves his father.

MENELAOS   And those who respect their mother?

ORESTES   Lucky them.

MENELAOS   Doesn't apply to you.

ORESTES   I don't care for bad women.

MENELAOS   Take your sword away from my daughter.

ORESTES   You're a tricky one aren't you.   [1240]

MENELAOS   You will really kill her!

ORESTES   You got that right.

MENELAOS   OIMOI! What should I do!

ORESTES   Go to the Argives and plead—

MENELAOS   What?

ORESTES   For our lives.

MENELAOS   Or you'll murder my child?

ORESTES   That's it.

MENELAOS   O poor Helen—

ORESTES   What about poor Orestes?   [1250]

MENELAOS   I brought you back from Troy unto death.

ORESTES   If only it were so.

MENELAOS   After all those toils—

ORESTES   None of them for me.

MENELAOS   I suffer terrible things.

ORESTES   Well, you screwed up.

MENELAOS   You've got me now.

ORESTES   You got yourself. You're no good, Menelaos.
    A born coward.
    Elektra, start that fire down below!
    Pylades, you light the parapet here.   [1260]

MENELAOS   O Argos, O citizens of Argos,
    won't you come to my rescue?
    This man is forcing his will upon your
        whole community—
    hanging on to life though he's soaked in his
        mother's blood!

[Enter APOLLO *with* HELEN, *above somewhere.]*

APOLLO   Menelaos, soften your temper—
    I am Phoibos Apollo, son of Leto, who calls
        you close at hand—
    you too, Orestes, with your sword at this
        girl's throat.

I have this to say.

Helen, whom you were so hot to kill,

is here. In the heavens.   [1270]

I saved her from your sword. Zeus' orders.

She is after all Zeus' daughter. Can't die.

She will sit in the folds of the sky beside
     Kastor and Pollux.

Sort of a savior for sailors.

Find another wife, Menelaos.

This one, by her beauty, was a mechanism of
     the gods

to kill off a lot of Trojans and Greeks,

lighten the burden of excess population on
     the earth.

So much for Helen.

Now you, Orestes,   [1280]

get out of this country. Cross the border,

go to Parrhasia, stay there a year.

They'll call the place *Oresteion* after you.

Then go to Athens and stand trial for
     matricide.

Trust me, you'll win.

And this girl whose throat is being grazed
     by your sword,

Hermione, you'll marry.

I know she's supposed to marry somebody
     else (Neoptolemos I think)

but I'll see to it he dies.

Give your sister to Pylades, as you agreed.   [1290]

His life will be happy.

And Argos—Menelaos—let Orestes rule it.
You go rule Sparta.
Enjoy your wife's dowry.
She's finished philandering now.
I'll fix up Orestes' relations with Argos—
it was me made him murder his mother
    after all.

ORESTES   Apollo of oracles! So you were no false
    prophet!
But I admit I was getting nervous.
Those voices, I thought they were demons
    of vengeance, not you!   [1300]
Still, it's all turned out well. I do obey
    you.
See, I'm letting Hermione go.
And will marry her as soon as her father says
    yes.

MENELAOS   Helen, daughter of Zeus, I hail you!
And congratulate you on your promotion
    to heaven!
Orestes, I give you the hand of my daughter.
    As Apollo ordains.
Noble bride, from a noble father,
I hope you prosper. I hope I do too.

APOLLO   Go your ways as I've assigned them.
End these differences.   [1310]

MENELAOS   No choice but to obey.

ORESTES   So it is.
           I make my peace with circumstances,
              Menelaos,
           and also with your oracles, Apollo.

APOLLO   Go then, honoring Peace, most beautiful of
              gods.
           I will lead Helen to the halls of Zeus
           crossing the starry bowl of the sky.
           There, with Hera and Herakles and Hebe,
           she will preside as a god,
           honored by humans,   [1320]
           queen of the deep running sea.

CHORUS   O great Victory, holy god,
           may you inhabit my life
           and never cease crowning me with beautiful
              success!